JOURNAL OF LEGAL PLURALISM and Unofficial Law

NUMBER 58 / 2008

CATALYZING THE SOCIO-LEGAL SPACE FOR ARMED CONFLICT: LAND AND LEGAL PLURALISM IN PRE-WAR LIBERIA
Jon Unruh

THE STRUGGLE FOR CONTEXT IN THE PROTECTION OF CHILDREN'S RIGHTS: UNDERSTANDING THE CORE CONCEPTS OF THE AFRICAN CHILDREN'S CHARTER
Thoko Khaime

'NEITHER FISH NOR FOWL': AREA COURTS IN THE ILORIN EMIRATE IN NORTHERN NIGERIA
Abdulmumuni A. Oba

FRAGMENTING LAND AND THE LAWS THAT GOVERN IT
Sue Farran

BOOK REVIEWS
Ralph Grillo
Gordon R. Woodman

Bibliographic information published by the Deutsche Nationalbibliothek
The Deutsche Nationalbibliothek lists this publication in the Deutsche Nationalbibliografie; detailed bibliographic data are available in the Internet at http://dnb.d-nb.de.

ISSN 0732-9113
ISBN 978-3-643-99932-0

A catalogue record for this book is available from the British Library

Fresnostr. 2 D-48159 Münster
Tel. +49 (0) 2 51-620 32 22 Fax +49 (0) 2 51-922 60 99
e-Mail: lit@lit-verlag.de http://www.lit-verlag.de

Distribution:

In Germany: LIT Verlag Fresnostr. 2, D-48159 Münster
Tel. +49 (0) 2 51-620 32 22, Fax +49 (0) 2 51-922 60 99, e-Mail: vertrieb@lit-verlag.de

In Austria: Medienlogistik Pichler-ÖBZ GmbH & Co KG
IZ-NÖ, Süd, Straße 1, Objekt 34, A-2355 Wiener Neudorf
Tel. +43 (0) 22 36-63 53 52 90, Fax +43 (0) 22 36-63 53 52 43, e-Mail: mlo@medien-logistik.at

In Switzerland: B + M Buch- und Medienvertriebs AG
Hochstr. 357, CH-8200 Schaffhausen
Tel. +41 (0) 52-643 54 30, Fax +41 (0) 52-643 54 35, e-Mail: order@buch-medien.ch

In the UK by: Global Book Marketing, 99B Wallis Rd, London, E9 5LN
Phone: +44 (0) 20 8533 5800 – Fax: +44 (0) 1600 775 663
http://www.centralbooks.co.uk/html

In North America by:

Transaction Publishers
New Brunswick (U.S.A.) and London (U.K.)

Transaction Publishers
Rutgers University
35 Berrue Circle
Piscataway, NJ 08854

Phone: +1 (732) 445 - 2280
Fax: + 1 (732) 445 - 3138
for orders (U. S. only):
toll free (888) 999 - 6778
e-mail: orders@transactionpub.com

JOURNAL OF LEGAL PLURALISM
and Unofficial Law

POLICY

The Journal of Legal Pluralism and Unofficial Law (JLP) is a refereed, independent, inter-disciplinary, international journal devoted to scholarly writing, documentation, information on current developments, and communications about all aspects of legal pluralism and unofficial law anywhere in the world and at any time. Issues 1-18 bear the name *African Law Studies*.

MANUSCRIPTS

Manuscripts for the Journal of Legal Pluralism should be submitted to the editor-in-chief:

Gordon R. Woodman
School of Law, University of Birmingham
Edgbaston, Birmingham B15 2TT
United Kingdom
Fax: (+ 44) (0)121 414 3585
Email: G.R.Woodman@bham.ac.uk

or to one of the associate editors. Unless the editors are otherwise informed, submission of a manuscript implies the undertaking that it is not currently being considered by another journal and that if accepted it will be available for publication.

Manuscripts must conform to the style and other instructions contained in the JLP 'style sheet' (to be found on the JLP web site under the title 'Author guidelines'), and should generally be submitted in electronic form.

SUBSCRIPTIONS

Subscriptions to the Journal of Legal Pluralism are currently €29.90 per number for individuals. Two numbers are published each year, the two amounting to approximately 200 pages. From nr. 49 (2004) the Journal has been published by LIT Verlag, Münster-Hamburg-Berlin-Vienna-London, whose address for orders is Grevener St./Fresnostr.2, D-48159 Münster, Germany, Fax (+49) (0)251 23 19 72, vertrieb@lit-verlag.de.

Back numbers of African Law Studies and the Journal of Legal Pluralism to nr. 48 are available from William S. Hein & Co., Inc., 1285 Main Street, Buffalo, New York 14209-1987, USA..

INDEXES AND DATABASES

Articles appearing in the Journal of Legal Pluralism are indexed in the principal legal and social science indexes and online data-bases. It is planned to make available the full text of all articles published more than two years previously on the website of the Journal of Legal Pluralism at www.jlp.bham.ac.uk . Currently the site contains the full text of all articles in nrs. 24 to 50, and abstracts of articles in nrs. 43 to the current number.

CITATION

The Journal of Legal Pluralism and Unofficial Law should be cited as: *Journal of Legal Pluralism*.

CONTENTS

FROM THE EDITORS vii

ABSTRACTS OF ARTICLES ix

ABOUT THE CONTRIBUTORS xv

CATALYZING THE SOCIO-LEGAL SPACE FOR ARMED CONFLICT: LAND AND LEGAL PLURALISM IN PRE-WAR LIBERIA
Jon Unruh 1

THE STRUGGLE FOR CONTEXT IN THE PROTECTION OF CHILDREN'S RIGHTS: UNDERSTANDING THE CORE CONCEPTS OF THE AFRICAN CHILDREN'S CHARTER
Thoko Khaime 33

'NEITHER FISH NOR FOWL': AREA COURTS IN THE ILORIN EMIRATE IN NORTHERN NIGERIA
Abdulmumuni A. Oba 69

FRAGMENTING LAND AND THE LAWS THAT GOVERN IT
Sue Farran 93

BOOK REVIEWS

Franz von Benda-Beckmann, Keebet von Benda-Beckmann, and Anne Griffiths (eds), *The Power of Law in a Transnational World: Anthropological Enquiries*. Oxford/New York: Berghahn Books. 2009
Ralph Grillo 115

Stephen Tierney (ed.), *Accommodating Cultural Diversity*. Aldershot UK and Burlington VT: Ashgate. 2007
Matthias Koenig and Paul de Guchteneire (eds.), *Democracy and Human Rights in Multicultural Societies*. Aldershot UK and Burlington VT: Ashgate. Paris: UNESCO. 2007

Prakash Shah and Werner F. Menski (eds.), *Migration, Diasporas and Legal Systems in Europe*. London and New York: Routledge-Cavendish. 2006.
Gordon R. Woodman 119

FROM THE EDITORS

This number opens with two papers which consider the relevance of legal pluralism to issues which are currently under much discussion both politically and in the socio-legal literature. Jon Unruh examines an aspect of Liberia's descent some years ago into internal armed conflict, considering the role of a disordered and dysfunctional legal pluralism in that decline. Thoko Khaime considers the concepts of children's universal rights and their relationship to the social reality of living law in an African society inspired by values which apparently diverge from those of international human rights, but which are seen on investigation to be quite possibly compatible with them. The other two papers document and discuss specific cases of legal pluralism in two states: Abdulmumuni Oba the case of the jurisdiction and functioning of Area Courts in the state of Ilorin in the Federal Republic of Nigeria; and Sue Farran the case of land law in the Pacific state of Vanuatu.

Sue Farran's article is developed from a paper presented at the recent international conference of the Commission on Legal Pluralism held in Zürich on *Legal Pluralist Perspectives on Development and Cultural Diversity*. We are pleased to publish this paper, and we expect to publish a number of others developed from papers presented at that conference, some in one or more special numbers on particular themes. Reports on the conference and other information about the Commission are available at http://www.commission-on-legal-pluralism.ch/. This is not to imply that we do not continue to receive, and warmly welcome, submissions of papers from other sources. Indeed, it is noteworthy how the range of authors and of subject-matter of papers submitted and published continues to grow. The study of legal pluralism and the exploration of the potential of the concepts of legal pluralism and unofficial law are in a hugely expansionist phase.

Gordon Woodman

ABSTRACTS OF ARTICLES

JLP 58: 1-31

CATALYZING THE SOCIO-LEGAL SPACE FOR ARMED CONFLICT:
LAND AND LEGAL PLURALISM IN PRE-WAR LIBERIA

Jon Unruh

Acutely antagonistic social relations involving land rights can be an important catalyst for armed conflict within countries of the developing world. When component parts of pluralistic socio-legal arrangements come to exist in opposition to one another, the result is a problematic buildup of confrontation, injustice, grievance, antipathy, and enmity. With no legitimate institutional way to deactivate the resulting tensions, they can become widespread and then volatile. This paper makes the argument that the way legal pluralism in land tenure is handled can be a significant contributor, if not a primary catalyst for armed conflict, and uses the case of Liberia to examine this. By analyzing the interaction of statutory, customary, 'state sponsored customary,' and *ad hoc* norms regarding land rights, the article describes how the very problematic socio-legal space with regard to land tenure was created in Liberia, and how interaction within this space was a primary catalyst for the war.

JOURNAL OF LEGAL PLURALISM
2008 - nr. 58

JLP 58: 33-67

THE STRUGGLE FOR CONTEXT IN THE PROTECTION OF CHILDREN'S RIGHTS: UNDERSTANDING THE CORE CONCEPTS OF THE AFRICAN CHILDREN'S CHARTER

Thoko Khaime

This article tries to escape orthodox analysis of children's rights analysis by engaging in a grounded examination of the core principles of Africa's core document on children's rights, the African Charter on the Rights and Welfare of the Child. There are four cross-cutting principles that may be thought of as underpinning the entire instrument. These are: the rule against discrimination; the 'best interests' rule; the rule promoting the child's survival and development; and the rule requiring the child's participation. The paper attempts to present a picture of these principles in action in the lives of the children and adults in areas of Southern Malawi where fieldwork was conducted among predominantly Lomwe people.

It is found that narratives that support *non-discrimination* perspectives are not only based on children's rights discourse but also on an eclectic mix of cultural, religious and spiritual arguments. Non-discrimination perspectives are not the preserve of human rights advocates alone but also that of ordinary people who claim no special knowledge of children's rights. Attempts to analyse the '*best interests*' principle encounter theoretical problems and difficulties of translation into the vernacular languages. It is found that, while there is a clear recognition that children's interests are an important issue in the management of the family, the customary processes for mediating those interests tend to serve interests 'larger' than those of the individual children. There is a clear acceptance of the *survival and development rights* of the child, but the manner in which these will be realised in relation to each individual child depends on the strength of the resource network to which such child has access, and in modern conditions some traditional resource networks are breaking down. *Participation rights* can be achieved by children using the channels of communication available in traditional society. Again changes in socio-economic patterns and the resultant mobility of rural folk have affected these, but it is concluded that arguments about the exact nature of the participation structures in the society studied are essentially non-fatal, and sooner or later there will be a resolution.

The article shows that, in seeking to determine the cultural legitimacy of the rights and welfare of the child, a methodology is required which focuses on detailed case studies so that an analysis of child rearing practice and its intersection with culture and children's rights is not formulated in abstract forms but is located in specific, concrete experiences derived from the lives of children and their families. The African Children's Charter's insistence on culture and context is supportive of this type of methodology which is sensitive to context, raises the legitimacy of the principles underlying the children's rights system, and gives rise to a pluralism that is neither universalist nor relativist but grounded in the reality of children's daily lives.

***JLP* 58: 69-92**

'NEITHER FISH NOR FOWL': AREA COURTS IN THE ILORIN EMIRATE IN NORTHERN NIGERIA

Abdulmumuni A. Oba

The Area Courts are the most heavily criticised of courts in Nigeria. They are frequently accused of incompetence, corruption, and arbitrariness. Another basic problem with the area courts is that of a crisis of identity. Law in Nigeria is a plural complex with English-style laws, Islamic law and customary laws operating to various extents. The Area Courts, although historically and basically Islamic law courts, partake of the other two laws. This paper assesses the extent to which the criticisms levelled against Area Courts hold true regarding those in the Ilorin Emirate in northern Nigeria.

The colonial system of indirect rule resulted in the preservation of the pre-existing Islamic Alkali courts, but a gradual assumption of control by the government. They were renamed Native Courts, and required to apply common law and customary laws as well as Islamic law. After Independence the courts were renamed Area Courts, but the system was continued.

Today Area Court judges are generally trained legal practitioners, and the courts are under the administrative control of the Chief Judge, also a trained legal practitioner. Legal practitioners represent litigants, and have brought the technicalities, delays and high costs of the common law into the system. Nevertheless, Area Court judges administering Islamic law generally think of themselves as Qadis and their courts as religious courts, and this is how the populace generally perceive them. Some results of this crisis of identity have been highhandedness, arbitrariness and corruption.

The paper concludes with suggestions of ways to improve the administration of justice in the Area Courts in Ilorin and in Northern Nigeria in general.

***JLP* 58: 93-113**

FRAGMENTING LAND AND THE LAWS THAT GOVERN IT

Sue Farran

In 1980 the Constitution of the newly independent Republic of Vanuatu returned all land to the custom owners and their descendants and declared that "[t]he rules of custom shall form the basis of ownership and use of land" (Articles 73 and 74). What the Constitution did not state was what these rules were or should be, leaving it to Parliament to implement a national land law. As a result of Parliamentary inaction there is a plurality of rules of custom which govern customary land tenure, varying from place to place and island to island in a country of over eighty islands. Traditionally these rules are unwritten, but increasingly they are being recorded, in the reports of courts and tribunals, in published research and in the policy documents of councils of chiefs. These are processes which in themselves are re-shaping the rules of custom but also providing a partial codification of customary practices. However, these are not the only rules which regulate land transactions. Introduced laws and post-independence national legislation are also important and exist alongside customary law. Different interests over the same land may therefore be regulated by different legal frameworks. Moreover the boundaries between these are shifting as land is used and developed in different ways to meet changing social and economic demands and pressures, both internal and external. There is therefore a pluralism of legal sources; a pluralism of values and concepts; and a pluralism of interests which in combination present substantial challenges for the articulation of a national land policy or the development a national land law.

This paper explores the nature of a plural land law and examines the potential for positive and negative outcomes in a rapidly changing environment in which land plays a pivotal role in the broader context of sustainable development and human rights.

ABOUT THE CONTRIBUTORS

Sue FARRAN is a Senior Lecturer in the School of Law at the University of Dundee, Scotland. She was formerly an Associate Professor of Law at the University of the South Pacific based in Vanuatu and continues to be a Visiting Lecturer there. Born in England, she received her legal education in South Africa (in Pietermaritzburg, Natal, and the University of South Africa) and at Cambridge, England, where she completed a BA in English and Social Anthropology in South Africa. She became a legal academic first in South Africa and then worked at the University of the West of England before moving to the South Pacific. The South Pacific region remains the focus of her research. Previous relevant publications include: *South Pacific Perspectives of Property Law.* London: Cavendish, 2003 (with D. Paterson); 'Conflicts of laws in Human Rights: Consequences for colonies.' *Edinburgh Law Review* 11: 121-126 (2007); 'Sand, Fish and Sea: A Legal Reflection on Islands - From Orkney to Vanuatu.' *International Journal of Coastal and Estuarine Law* 21: 389-421 (2006); 'Human Rights in the Pacific Region - Challenges and Solutions.' *LAWASIA Journal* 39-68 (2005); 'Land Rights and Gender Equality in the Pacific Region.' *Australian Property Law Journal* 11: 131-140 (2005). Her most recent book is: *Human Rights in the South Pacific: Challenges and Changes*. London: Routledge-Cavendish (2009).

Ralph GRILLO received a PhD degree in anthropology at the University of Cambridge in 1968. He lectured at Queen's University Belfast (1967-70), and subsequently at the University of Sussex, where he was Dean of the School of African and Asian Studies, and founding Director of the Graduate Research Centre for the Study of Culture, Development and the Environment. He has conducted anthropological field research in East Africa, Ireland, France and Italy. While now retired he remains active in research and writing. While he has written previously on the anthropology of development and the anthropology of language, his principal concern now is with transnational migration and multiculturalism in Europe, and contemporary debates about culture in this context. Some of his more recent books and journal special issues are: (edited, with B. Soares), 'Islam, Transnationalism and the Public Sphere in Western Europe'. Special Issue of *Journal of Ethnic and Migration Studies* 30(5) (2004); (with V. Mazzucato), 'Africa< >Europe: Transnational Linkages, Multi-sited Lives.' Special Issue of *Journal of Ethnic and Migration Studies* 34(2) (2008); (ed.), *The Family in Question: Immigrant and Ethnic Minorities in Multicultural Europe*. Amsterdam: Amsterdam University

Press (2008); and (edited, with R. Ballard, A. Ferrari, A.J. Hoekema, M. Maussen and P. Shah), *Legal Practice and Cultural Diversity*. Aldershot: Ashgate (2009).

Thoko KHAIME is a member of the Law, Environment and Development Centre of the School of Law, School of Oriental and African Studies, University of London. He has studied law at the Universities of Malawi, Pretoria and Western Cape, and holds the degrees of LLM from the University of Pretoria, and PhD from the University of London. He conducts research in the fields of international law, human rights, children's rights, and law and natural resources, primarily in Africa. His recent publications are: 'The protection of refugee children under the African human rights system: finding durable solutions in international law.' Pp. 183-197 in Julia Sloth-Nielsen (ed.), *Children's Rights in Africa: A Legal Perspective*. London: Ashgate (2008); 'Socio-legal approaches to children's rights under the African Charter on the Rights and Welfare of the Child: A discussion of methodology.' Pp. 255-274 in Bill Atkin (ed.), *The International Survey of Family Law* 2009 Edition. Bristol : Family Law (2009). Currently in press is his: *The African Charter on the Rights and Welfare of the Child: A socio-legal perspective*. Pretoria: Pretoria University Law Press.

Abdulmumuni A. OBA, LL. B., LL. M., B.L., is a Senior Lecturer in the Faculty of Law, University of Ilorin, Ilorin, Nigeria and was Head, Department of Jurisprudence and International Law 1998 - 2002 (E-mail: obailorin@yahoo.com). He has published extensively on the fields of constitutional law, administration of Islamic law and Customary Law in Nigeria, human rights, and Comparative Law which are the major areas of his research interest. His more recent publications include "Rethinking Legal Education in Nigeria" *Journal of Commonwealth Law and Legal Education*, Vol. 6 No. 1, 2008, 97, "Female Circumcision as Female Genital Mutilation: Human Rights or Cultural Imperialism?" *Global Jurists* Vol. 8, Iss. 3 (*Frontiers*) 2008, Article 8, pp. 1 - 38 and "Juju Oaths in Customary Law Arbitration and their Legal Validity in Nigerian Courts" *Journal of African Law* Vol. 52, No. 1, 2008, 139–158.

Jon UNRUH is a Professor of Geography at McGill University in Montreal. His research, applied, and policy work over the past 20 years has dealt with post-conflict land and property rights in the developing world, and the intersection of land tenure and environmental change. His past endeavors have focused on conflict resolution, land policy and law, restitution, legal pluralism, approaches to reconciling customary and formal tenure systems, and agriculture in postwar and peace-building scenarios. His experience includes work in Liberia, Somalia, Mozambique, East Timor, Sierra Leone, Liberia, Zanzibar, Ethiopia, Uganda, Madagascar, and Colombia. He has a Ph.D. in geography from the University of Arizona, a Masters degree from the University of Wisconsin-Madison, and an undergraduate degree from the University of Kansas-Lawrence. Some of his recent publications include: 'Land policy reform, customary rule of law and the peace process in Sierra Leone.' *African Journal of Legal Studies* 2: 94-117 (2008); 'Carbon sequestration in Africa: the land tenure problem.' *Global Environmental Change: Human and Policy Dimensions* 18: 700-707 (2008); 'Land tenure and the "evidence landscape" in developing countries.' *Annals of the Association of American Geographers* 96: 754-772; 'Toward sustainable livelihoods after war: reconstituting rural land tenure systems.' *Natural Resources Forum* 32: 103-115; (with N.C. Heynen and P. Hossler), 'The political ecology of recovery from armed conflict: the case of landmines in Mozambique.' *Political Geography* 22: 841-861 (2003).

Gordon R. WOODMAN is editor-in-chief of the *Journal of Legal Pluralism* and Emeritus Professor of Comparative Law at Birmingham Law School, University of Birmingham, England. His recent publications include: (ed., with Rubya Mehdi, Hanne Petersen and Erik Sand), *Law and Religion in Multicultural Societies*, Copenhagen: DJØF Publishing (2008); (ed., with Diethelm Klippel), *Risk and the Law*. Abingdon: Routledge-Cavendish (2008); 'From Alien Intruder to Nation's Monarch to International Agent: The Changing Roles of the African State in the Realm of Law.' Pp. 187-204 in Reinhard Zimmermann (ed.), *Globalisierung und Entstaatlichung des Rechts – Teilband 2: Nichtstaatliches Privatrecht: Geltung und Genese,* Tübingen: Mohr Siebeck (2008); 'The Culture Defence in English Common Law: The Potential for Development.' Pp. 7-34 in Marie-Claire Foblets and Alison Dundes Renteln (eds.), *Multicultural Jurisprudence: Comparative Perspectives on the Cultural Defense,* Oxford and Portland Oregon: Hart Publishing (2009); (with Maarten Bavinck), 'Can There Be Maps Of Law?' Pp. 195-218 in Franz von Benda-Beckmann, Keebet von Benda-Beckmann and Anne Griffiths (eds.), *Spatialising Law: An Anthropological Geography of Law in Society*, Farnham Britain and Burlington VT: Ashgate (2009); 'The Challenge of African Customary Laws to English Legal Culture.' Chap. 8, pp. 135-150 in Ralph Grillo, Roger Ballard, Alessandro Ferrari, André J. Hoekema, Marcel Maussen and Prakash Shah (eds.), *Legal Practice and Cultural Diversity*, Aldershot: Ashgate (2009).

CATALYZING THE SOCIO-LEGAL SPACE FOR ARMED CONFLICT: LAND AND LEGAL PLURALISM IN PRE-WAR LIBERIA

Jon D. Unruh

Introduction

While acute land rights problems are recognized as an important catalyst for armed conflict, precisely what the structural-tenurial catalyzing process comprises, remains unexamined. Aggressively confrontational social relations involving land rights emerge from a pluralistic socio-legal space in which the component parts come to be set against one another. The result is an aggravated accumulation of competition, inequity, confrontation, grievance, resentment, and animosity, with no institutional way to manage these across opposing components. This paper makes the argument that while the interface between customary and statutory land tenure is a problem in many parts of Africa, the way such legal pluralism is handled can be a significant contributor to armed conflict. While many countries contain some variation of a pluralistic customary–statutory tenure divide, it is treated and managed in a wide variety of ways. Liberia's approach prior to its civil war (occurring in two phases, 1989-1996 and 1999-2003) was to engage in a form of divisive pluralism in the country's constitutional, social, political, economic, and institutional life from the beginning of its history as a country (Richards et al. 2004). The distinctions made between 'civilized' and 'uncivilized' peoples, laws, customs, culture, and importantly land tenure, had a pervasive, long-term, and polarizing influence in the interaction of different sets of land rights. Ultimately the tenurial socio-legal space in Liberia comprised an extremely aggravated interaction which led to an agrarian crisis constituting the wholesale failure of rural institutions; a crisis which Richards et al. (2004) articulately describe.

It is widely acknowledged that land problems were a primary factor in the cause and maintenance of the war in Liberia and the ensuing crisis (e.g. GRC 2007; Bruce 2007; Richards 2005; Sawyer 2005; ICG 2006; Banks 2007; Kollie 2006; Wily 2007; Unruh 2009). Indeed Bruce (2007) notes that early battles over land erupted due to fundamental differences in conceptions of land ownership between the Americo-Liberian settlers and indigenous inhabitants as early as 1822, the year Liberia was founded. Riddell and Dickerman (1986, 102), citing Liebnow, note that during the Doe regime (1980-1990) "[l]and tenure is at the heart of rural discontent." Subsequent to the war, the Liberian Governance Reform Commission concluded that access to land was a root cause of the armed conflict (GRC 2007). However how this 'root cause' came about has not yet been examined adequately.

This article describes how the socio-legal space with regard to land tenure was created in Liberia, and how interaction within this space was a primary catalyst for the war. The interaction between a contradictory and confused set of formal land laws, strongly held customary concepts about land, discriminatory 'state sponsored' customary law, and numerous *ad hoc* land and property norms connected to instability, constituted the socio-legal space within which extremely volatile tensions came to reside. With no legitimate way to deactivate these tensions, they became pervasive and then explosive. Subsequent to a description of the fieldwork and the legislation examined, this paper describes the background to the Liberian case, defines the socio-legal space by briefly specifying the different bodies of formal and informal law, and then analyzes the relevant patterns of socio-legal interaction.

Data Gathering

The research for this analysis comprised a series of individual and group interviews and focus group discussions in Liberia totaling 210 people in the months of December 2006 and February 2007, as part of land tenure policy reform work led by the Liberian Governance Reform Commission. Those interviewed included smallholder farmers, large landholders, ministry officials, university researchers, NGOs, lawyers, UN personnel, commercial agriculture associations, bilateral and multilateral donors, international legal and development organizations, and a former President of the country. The laws analyzed include: The Constitution 1986, The Public Lands Law 1956, The Local Government Law 1972, Laws and Regulations Governing the Hinterland revised 2001, Rules and Regulations

Governing Local Government Officials revised 2005,[1] The Wildlife and National Parks Act 1987, and The Natural Resources Law 1999. As well an examination of the relevant academic, Liberian government, NGO, legal, and donor literature took place.

Background

Former American slaves were settled on the Liberian coast beginning in the 19th century, and a statutory system of land tenure was established in areas under their control. The settler society was exclusive, and resided within an array of indigenous African coastal communities. These indigenous communities possessed land tenure systems that held land to be inalienable. Nevertheless settlers interacting with local communities pursued alienation of land (instead of use) made possible by a mix of violent conflict and alliance-making (Sawyer 2005). Settler acquisition of lands was supported by a variety of (largely received) laws, including an early constitution (Sawyer 2005; Wily 2007). While indigenous lands on the coast appear to have been purchased, in the 'hinterland' indigenous land was acquired through an extension of the 1847 constitution into the interior, together with its enabling laws (Wily 2007). Indigenous customary law, based on usufruct rights, continued in areas inhabited by local communities and administered as provinces by the Liberian state. The initial decades of the 20th century saw often brutal subjugation of parts of the countryside, with the resulting tensions between the settlers and indigenous inhabitants reflected in longstanding land issues. When the provinces became counties in the mid-twentieth century, the customary tenure system continued, and parts of it became 'sponsored' (meaning officialized, altered and used by the state), while other parts were neglected or declared illegal (GRC 2007).

Indigenous smallholder claim and use of land was the tenurial focus of most of the Liberian interior until Firestone was established as the first rubber concession in the 1920s (GRC 2007). The statutory tenure system then became the legal basis for the derivation of concessions for rubber, timber, and minerals throughout the country. Such concessions were often foreign-controlled private commercial farms.

[1] The Laws and Regulations Governing the Hinterland and the Local Government Officials Law were only very slightly revised toward the end of the war, and thus continue to exist largely in their prewar states.

Over time, increasing areas of rural Liberia were transferred from the customary system to the statutory tenure system by the acquisition of land deeds by Americo-Liberians using state sponsored customary law through chiefs (GRC 2007). Enormous land acquisitions deprived local inhabitants of access to agricultural land, sacred groves, shrines, and tree crops (Bruce 2007). Rampant land appropriation and land speculation eventually evolved into sources of acute uncertainty, grievance and conflict. By the outbreak of the civil war in 1990, the legal mechanisms for acquiring land deeds, especially in areas under forms of customary tenure, was a seriously contentious and volatile issue (Unruh 2009; GRC 2007). This included mechanisms for acquiring rights to lands which contained valuable timber and alluvial diamond and gold deposits which fueled the conflict (UNEP 2004).

The Tenurial Legal Fields: Formal, Customary, 'State Sponsored Customary', and ad hoc Norms

This section briefly describes the primary components which comprised the socio-legal space regarding land tenure in pre-war Liberia. The functioning and interaction of these components within this space is then examined in the subsequent section.

Formal land law in Liberia

Liberia's statutory law resides within the Anglo-American common law legal tradition. As a new country in the early 1800s Liberia 'received' a complex body of statutory land law from the United States initially derived in England and modified over decades to suit American social reality (Bruce 2007). Particularly relevant in the Liberian context, is that American law regarding land and indigenous people in the early 1800s was extremely discriminatory in its treatment of land rights (Unruh 2002). The degree and effectiveness of the subsequent modification of this law by Liberian legal decisions and statutes in order to serve Liberian reality, was profoundly inadequate. There was also a great deal of confusion regarding the overall status and application of Liberian derived polices and laws regarding land and property. Those that existed were unclear, often contradictory, lacked effective implementing regulations, and for most of the country's history were very dated and so did not effectively engage contemporary

Liberia.[2] Bruce (2007) notes that the lack of access to court decisions and laws in Liberia before the war was so severe that it constituted a legal vacuum.

Prior to the conflict there existed five primary statutory laws in Liberia that defined formal land rights and the relationship (from a statutory perspective) between formal and customary tenure systems. While two of these laws were central to how statutory land rights worked, and contained articles that pertained to the interface between statutory and customary tenure (The Constitution 1986, The Public Lands Law 1956), three others were focused almost entirely on interaction between the formal and customary sectors (Local Government Law 1972, Laws and Regulations Governing the Hinterland revised 2001, Rules and Regulations Governing Local Government Officials revised 2005). Two additional laws were also relevant to the interface between tenure systems, the Wildlife and National Parks Act 1987, and the Natural Resources Law 1999.

In the period leading up to the war there was significant ambiguity, confusion, and contradiction regarding which laws were to have been applied in which cases and how, particularly with regard to the granting of concessions and resolution of disputes. As well, the court system constituted a problematic and pluralistic set of institutions for solving land and property disputes, and there existed an extremely confused variety of procedures for dispute resolution depending on the actors, the context, and the issue at hand. The overall perspective of statutory land-related laws, beginning with the Constitution, was that the customary inhabitant of Liberia was subject to statutory laws, while not being able to participate in them—meaning they possessed little in the way of constitutional rights, resulting in an inability to hold land under statutory law. At the same time Americo-Liberians were not subject to customary laws. This set the formal tenure system against the customary system, which the government attempted to resolve by the delimitation of 'state sponsored customary law', but which instead created a third tenure system.

[2] Much in Liberian statutory law regarding land, prior to the war, reflected colonial approaches that did not resonate with contemporary social realities (Bruce 2007), even within the formal tenure system. For example the Laws and Regulations for Governing the Hinterland is almost the same in both structure and language to other Anglophone African colonies in West Africa that date from the 1930s and 1940s, which have in those countries been abandoned and revised, while Liberia has maintained them (ICG 2006).

Customary legal concepts about land

Customary law in Liberia and land tenure in particular is exceptionally poorly documented and studied, as are how any customary tenure cases might have been handled by statutory courts, and the interactions between customary and civil authorities (Bruce 2007; ICG 2006). Allot (1967), writing during one of the brief periods when the *Liberian Law Journal* was publishing, noted that "[p]ractically no cases involving the substantive rules of customary law have ever reached the Liberian law reports". In particular the issues of when to apply customary or statutory law and the conflict of laws "has received little if any legislative or judicial attention" (Allot 1967). As well McCarthy's (2007) review of Liberian Supreme Court cases found almost none mentioning customary land law. Bruce (2007: 28) notes that '[t]here is perhaps no country in Africa where less is known of customary systems of land tenure". Thus this section of the article instead of describing customary land law in Liberia, describes from the fieldwork two broad fundamental customary legal concepts, or postulates regarding land, that are not a set of customary laws per se, but are nonetheless very strongly held and defended, and are what customary tenure laws are based on.

The first concept is that customary group connection to specific land areas in Liberia is based on the idea of early and later arrivals. The distinction between groups (including their descendents) who arrived first in certain areas of the country, and the chronology of the founding of particular settlements, versus those who arrived later, is a primary customary land concept that serves as a foundation for other customary legal prescriptions. Widely practiced in West Africa (e.g. Marshall-Fratani 2006; Eboh 2005; Jackson 2006; Kuba and Lentz 2006) such a distinction drives subsequent customary laws regarding descent, belonging, and attachment to groups and lands. Such descent laws are then used to exclude outsiders or restrict in certain ways their rights to land. 'First-comers' in this context are believed to have almost ultimate legitimacy in a customary sense, to rights to land. In many cases this concept provides the basis for those in the 'first-comer' group to make laws affecting the transfer of land, inclusion and exclusion of others, and what rights various segments of local inhabitants have and do not have; such as the right to build houses, farm, plant trees, and bury the dead. In some cases the first comer group only includes a particular lineage (descendents of the founders), but in other cases it can be extended to include an entire ethnic group. The fieldwork noted that while the first-comers refer to the deeds of their ancestors as the legitimizing property constituting acts (discovery of the land in question, settlement or its conquest, or pacts with the gods or spirits, etc) late comers can also claim land by such acts (usually by clearing land, albeit the claim is weaker). Such acts legitimize, at least in the mind of those engaged in such acts, occupation, claim, and the right to control the activities of others on the land in question. More broadly, first comer-late comer aspects of claims to land in a variety of constructs are fairly widespread, figuring prominently in issues of ethno-nationality (Engerman et al. 2004), migration (Landau 2006), autochthony and colonization (Ceuppens 2006), history of landscapes (Russell 1997), and identity (Herb and Kaplan 1999).

The second postulate is the customary belief that land cannot be subdivided or inherited privately, and that lineage lands belong to the dead, living, and unborn. In some locations this is stronger than others, and in an increasing number of locations it is re-emerging as a significantly strong 'invoked law', as it is elsewhere in Africa (e.g. Geschiere and Jackson 2006; Eboh 2005; Leynseele and Nebinck 2009; Fay 2009). Under this arrangement, land rights are vested in communities and are prohibited from sale. The 'community' may be families, a tribe, a clan, or villages. The head of the community then decides the basis for allocating land to community members (also Kollie 2006). Land that has been gained or allocated to lineage families is generally held by them in perpetuity, or at least internal to the lineage and chiefdom.[3]

State sponsored customary law

A significant aspect of the institutionalized separation of tenure systems in the country was the delimitation of 'state sponsored' customary law. This comprised certain subsets of customary law that became state sanctioned, supported, controlled, altered, and formally legitimized. This officially recognized customary law deviated from indigenous laws and in particular how they operated, to the degree that there existed competition between state sponsored and indigenous customary tenure and laws (Bruce 2007). For example the fieldwork revealed that a 'clan' in state sponsored customary law was not based on the idea of lineage as it existed in indigenous customary law, but was instead a geographic administrative area. As a result, the operative notion of clan in much of the interior eventually changed into a geographical area with a kin aspect. However in many locations there seemed to be little correspondence between the geographic area under the

[3] Such a right of holding however does not traditionally include the right to alienate land, or hold it privately (see for example, Bropleh 1989).

state sponsored definition of clan area, and the lineages' customary idea of traditional lands.

The government sought to ensure that state sponsored customary law would govern 'natives', while statutory law would govern Americo-Liberians, missionaries, and immigrants; although again 'natives' were subject to statutory law. From the fieldwork it was noted that this historical institutionalized divide was a primary source of subsequent tensions and acute problems (described later). The primary law articulating state sponsored customary law with regard to land, was the lengthy and substantively very dated 'Law and Regulations Governing the Hinterland'. Also important however, to setting this domain of law against others, was what was defined by the state as non-sanctioned and illegal customary law, together with customary laws which were simply ignored or loosely tolerated.

There were also a number of customary law-making institutions, which were not sanctioned by the state, and depending on the institution, were either prohibited or partially controlled. The Law of the Hinterland allowed some Poro and Sande secret societies as 'cultural societies', albeit under some control.[4] Specifically noted as 'unlawful societies' were six other secret societies and all societies of a political nature.[5] But because land tenure is always political this greatly aggravated the relationship between state sponsored customary law and indigenous customary law. As well, 'house palavers' in which disputes between extended family members are resolved by the oldest males, were not state sponsored and essentially ignored in statutory law (ICG 2006).

ad hoc land and property norms

Different from indigenous customary law which develops over considerable time, *ad hoc* land and property norms, as defined here, can emerge over a much shorter period in reaction to a combination of: confusion about laws, lack of enforcement, inequity (in both formal and customary law), and a variety of other land problems. The result is a reluctance to follow tenure rules that others are not following, and a

[4] For example permission was needed from the District Commissioner prior to their establishment (GoL 2001, article 68).

[5] The six illegal societies are: the Human Leopard Society, the Negee Society, Suska, Toya, Kala, and Uama-Yama.

hence a search for alternative 'normative orders' (e.g., Merry 1988; Griffiths 1986). Such informal 'legalities', while somewhat similar to what Plunkett (2005) calls informal 'micro rule of law systems' for postwar scenarios, and what Moore (1973) describes as 'semi-autonomous social fields' for stable settings, are different in that they comprise a variety of relatively quickly constituted alternative approaches to acquiring, (re)establishing, securing, defending, and proving rights and claims to property, land, homeland, and territory during unstable socio-political conditions—in Liberia's case the years leading up to the war. Their derivation parallels the general fracturing of society into smaller communities of shared experience, dislocation, and disaffection during times of considerable stress, instability, and state malfunction. In such a situation, *ad hoc* land and property norms that are incompatible, opposed, or in aggregate add confusion, confrontation and tenure insecurity, can significantly aggravate the socio-legal space of land tenure.

In Liberia the fieldwork found that the increasing instability of both customary and formal law prior to the war resulted in the emergence of a variety of aggressively pursued *ad hoc* norms tied to specific groups, which facilitated the claim, acquisition, and protection of lands. These groups were often opposed to each other and included: disenfranchised rural youth (with large numbers becoming combatants); dislocatees and squatters unable to access land or deprived of their lands; women's groups; specific ethnic groups and their subdivisions; opportunists claiming access and exploitation rights to land-based resources such as timber, rubber, and alluvial mineral deposits; opportunists in government able to access and alter land records; landholders acting to sell land and property held in fee simple multiple times; and chiefs and elders acting under the auspices of state sponsored customary law together with bribes, to sell customary land to outsiders, and coercively extract land and labor from rural youth or prevent land from being allocated to them. As well there was an adherence of certain groups to forms of Islamic law, particularly in the northeast of the country, in this case not as an *ad hoc* norm, but rather a readily available alternative.

Patterns of Socio-Legal Interaction

Within Liberia's pre-war socio-legal space, there existed four primary patterns of interaction with regard to the sets of land rights 'legalities' that were most problematic: separation and isolation; ambiguity and confusion; the emergence of ad hoc land and property norms; and customary tenure versus statutory and state sanctioned customary law. While certain aspects of these patterns are also present in other countries, in Liberia all aspects of these patterns were present together, and were responsible for the creation of acute and volatile tensions in land tenure, which in aggregate contributed significantly to the onset of the war. This section describes these patterns, how they came about, and how they operated prior to the war to become explosive.

Separation and isolation

A primary relationship between law and society in the common law legal tradition (and many others, including customary traditions), operates through mutual exposure and the legal and societal change that occurs over time as a result of this exposure, so that law serves and is connected to society as it changes (e.g., Delville 2003; Andre 2003; McAuslan 1998; Platteau 2000). The fieldwork found that this is important to the Liberia case in two ways. First, the purposeful and maintained separation and isolation of formal and customary tenure, and second, the failure of Liberian formal legal institutions to update statutory law. Thus while there were distinct statutory laws for treating Americo-Liberians and indigenous Liberians separately, because the two groups did in reality interact 'on-the-ground' over issues of land, how this interaction occurred in the absence of statutory constructs relating to the interaction was crucial to the effect of law on Liberian society.

(a) statutory-customary separation and isolation

Current understanding regarding the disconnect between formal and customary land tenure in the developing world holds that the 'adaptation paradigm' is a significantly important way forward in the co-adaptation of the two systems (Bruce and Migot-Adholla 1994). This co-adaptation occurs over time and involves not only the recognition and accommodation of customary ways by formal law, but the evolutionary transformation of customary law as well, in reaction to interaction with formal law. In a number of developing countries the exposure and influence between tenure systems is encouraged, is significant, and serves to bring new ideas, innovation, and adaptability to problems pertaining to customary and statutory interaction, land laws, and tenurial situations.[6] In pre-war Liberia

[6] For example Delville (2003) observes in several countries (Rwanda, Ivory Coast,

however the two systems were acknowledged to be distinct (not a real problem in itself, as this occurs in many locations in Africa) and that they were to be kept separate and not interact (the real problem). Thus there was little borrowing of ideas, issues, logic, experiences, methods, etc., (co-adaptation) over time between the two tenure systems in a legally progressive sense. Bruce (2007) notes for Liberia specifically that "[t]he failure to process customary land law disputes in the courts has important and negative implications for the evolution of customary land law. In other common law jurisdictions in Africa, customary rules have been reviewed and groomed by the courts for absorption into a larger body of common law. There has in Liberia been no such process". The fieldwork revealed that instead the opposite occurred. As opposed to forms of customary and formal law becoming integrated, they were set against one another, and this is quite different than in other African states. For example, both the 'Laws and Regulations Governing the Hinterland' revised 2001, and the 'Rules and Regulations Governing Local Government Officials' were revised toward the end (Hinterland law in 2001) and after the war (Local Government Officials law in 2005), but because of the lack of exposure to customary laws, they are largely unchanged from their previous versions, thus retaining highly discriminatory aspects of law that were known to be connected to the cause of the war from the customary perspective. The result of such mutual isolation was an ongoing pluralism in a divisive way that generated and aggravated disputes as participants in both tenure systems interacted with each other over land access, claim, control, and exploitation. Thus the institution of 'state-sponsored customary law' in Liberia, and its intention to replace indigenous customary law, together with the purposeful isolation between indigenous customary and formal tenure, explicitly did not allow for indigenous customary law to penetrate and influence statutory law, or the reverse.

The fieldwork noted that what made this lack of exposure increasingly volatile over time for Liberia was that there were areas of very problematic and unresolved contradiction between indigenous customary, state sponsored customary, and

Benin, Senegal) the infiltration of formal-like evidence (various forms of informal documentation) and procedures into customary land law that attest to land transactions (also Andre 2003). And there have been a number of cases elsewhere in Africa of the hybridizing of formal and informal land tenure systems, with significantly positive results in integrating the two (e.g. Bruce 2007; Maganga 2003; McAuslan 1998; Okoth-Ogendo 2000; Platteau 2000; Toulmin and Quan 2000).

formal law. The Constitution, the Hinterland Law, and the Public Lands Law are three examples where fundamental customary concepts regarding 'first comers,' inalienability, property constituting acts, group membership, and boundary,[7] were violated, with no institution, legal construct, or mechanism able to legitimately reconcile contradictions. Especially problematic were provisions within laws (regarding public lands, ownership of forests, the hinterlands), that claimed land belonged to the state, when such lands had clearly been occupied and used for very long periods of time under customary law. Such claims were a primary source of the tensions that contributed to the war (Bruce 2007). The Land Law of 1956 for example primarily attended to Americo-Liberian settlers in areas they occupied. All other land in the interior was, and continues to be, primarily occupied by indigenous Africans under customary land tenure, but is legally considered the property of the state and therefore public land (World Bank 2007). At the same time indigenous, non-Christian Africans were unable to use the Land Law themselves and the customary courts and their chiefs could not hear a case to which a 'civilized' person was a party (ICG 2006).

While Liberian statutory law acted to keep formal and customary tenure separate, those operating within customary tenure also acted to keep the two distinct, albeit for different reasons and in a different way. The fieldwork revealed that there existed significant resistance by those following customary tenure to the discriminatory statutory laws and practices (including state sponsored customary law). This acted to restrict the penetration of potentially valuable aspects of formal law into customary law. For example, the ongoing use of 'trial by ordeal' (described later) and 'invoked law' regarding return to the lineage of previously sold land, reveals a lack of exposure to what statutory laws are about. And while Poro secret societies were of some utility for land tenure including enforcement of decisions, at the same time the secret nature of these societies presented a significant constraint to the 'back and forth' exchange of information, ideas, and legal innovations necessary for customary tenure to evolve. And because

[7] 'Soap trees' are the primary boundary marker for the customary sector throughout Liberia. The tree doesn't grow by itself, but must be planted. It does not seed, but puts up a number of trunks from one root system, creating a stand of trees. According to smallholders it is also accepted by formal law as evidence of a boundary location, and therefore ownership—although it is not specifically noted in formal law. Other terrain features are also used for customary boundaries: rivers, hills, etc. but these do not carry the evidentiary weight that soap trees do.

membership or participation in other secret or political societies,[8] and customary laws and institutions that were deemed illegal could be severely punished, including with imprisonment (GoL 2001, article 68), this encouraged their secret nature, their resistance to formal law, and their operation in isolation.

An additional factor acting to keep customary and formal tenure systems separate was the capacity of the formal legal system. The common law tradition in Liberia allowed judges to consider a broad range of sources in making legal decisions, including testimony and use of witnesses regarding how customary law works. In this regard there was applicability of customary law in statutory courts (also Bruce 2007). However in practice the profound failure of these components of the legal system to build a known body of customary - formal law interaction contributed significantly to their isolation. This was in part due to the low capacity of the formal legal establishment over time, along with its rigidity and over-formalistic notions of law. This deterministic mindset was, prior to the war, unwilling to receive input from the customary sector in terms of legal development of the country. Integrity of statutory law was, and continues to be, valued over 'law and society'. Contributing further to this problem, was the lack of operating lower courts; the distance between such courts and most rural or town inhabitants; and the lack of literacy, knowledge, and finances needed to file cases. As well the strong American ties, and prolonged organizational and institutional privation in successive governments made importing laws from elsewhere easier than developing Liberian-specific laws able to effectively embrace the interface between customary and statutory law in land tenure.

(b) received and outdated formal law

In the Western legal tradition, the role of legal journals or national law reports serve to inform the development of statutory law as an ongoing exercise (e.g., McAuslan 2003; Bruce 2007). This occurs by making known to lawyers, judges and the law-making process in general, what is important to society and how to address these. The lack in Africa however of "a national legal literature of some intellectual depth and maturity" (McAuslan 2003: 53) has both hindered the

[8] The connection between the illegality of political societies, and the reality that land tenure is always political (Bruce and Migot-Adholla 1994) contributed to driving customary tenure activities into a hidden, and isolated domain of customary interaction.

development of the relationship between laws and social realities (including customary law), and instead has continued or enhanced the influence of European and American law (McAuslan 2003). The fieldwork revealed that there was little attempt in Liberia at localization of these laws. Particularly relevant in Liberia's case, is McAuslan's (2003: 61) work, which concludes that for Anglophone African countries "the influence [of received law] has grown since independence; with the collapse in so many countries of a system of national law reports, judges rely on precedents from English and South African law reports which continue to be received in the law court libraries in lieu of anything else". In Liberia's case The *Liberian Law Journal* started publishing only in 1965 (143 years after the country was founded), stopped publishing from 1970-1974, resumed for a few issues, stopped again, published once more in 1986, then stopped permanently due to the problems developing in the country, and has yet to resume after the war.

As an example of the large role of received law in Liberia, reference is made in the Public Lands Law (GoL1956, article 90) to the government held right of 'escheat', which is the "reversion of property to the state in consequence of a want of any individual competent to inherit" (Black 1991). The definition of escheat focuses on the 'competent individual' as opposed to a group, able to inherit land. The fieldwork noted however that rural land in the Liberian interior is in most cases tied to groups and not individuals, with indigenous individuals unable to inherit land in the individualized Western sense. Instead land is tied to the lineage and access to it by lineage members is subject to clan, Paramount Chief, and elders' prescriptions. In the Public Lands Law the procedure for reclaiming land back from the government that it has taken over via the right of escheat is also focused on the individual, and assumes a good deal of literacy and financial resources.[9] Thus because customary groups do not pursue inheritance based on the individual, this aspect of the law is unworkable, goes against customary concepts of the group-land relationship, and resulted in loss of land and a source of grievance.

Ambiguity and confusion

From the fieldwork it emerged that the pervasive ambiguity and confusion on the

[9] Financial resources are necessary because the "deed shall be delivered only after the claimant shall have refunded to the Government the amount of any commission paid to the County, Territorial, or District Attorney on the escheat of the property" (Public Lands Law 1956e).

part of both customary and formal tenure participants that was generated by the legal regime in Liberia prior to the war had a primary impact on tenure security. In a numerous of areas in the country customary owners are so insecure that they prohibit renters from planting trees or making other investments in land, believing that these will lead to claims. Widespread insecurity also turned many people away from adhering to either formal or customary law when neither provided clarity or effective tenure security. At the same time such ambiguity was an opportunity in that, in such a volatile, socio-politically unpredictable environment as pre-war Liberia, ambiguity was a strategy employed by some to acquire or preserve tenuous rights of land occupation, ownership, and use. Chiefs used the ambiguity and uncertainty created by state sponsored customary law and its competition with indigenous customary law to acquire large amounts of land and free labor that would not have been possible otherwise. Ambiguity was also quite valuable for opportunists operating within formal law seeking to obtain or retain land and property fraudulently, or sell the same land multiple times. Chabal and Daloz (1999) comment at length on the utility of such ambiguity and disorder as a tool elsewhere in Africa.

While there was a breadth of ambiguity-generating sources in statutory law regarding land rights, two laws were particularly problematic. The Liberian Constitution articulates the division between customary law and statutory law generally, but then refers specifically only to 'property' in the formal private property sense (GoL 1986), thus apparently applying only to those not from rural native areas. The result was to leave in an indeterminate state the ultimate, final rights of those from the interior. Such ambiguity acted to allow a wide range of manipulations, expropriation, and other conversions of 'non-private' holdings into private holdings; a conversion which aboriginal inhabitants were themselves unable to participate in.

Significantly ambiguous in the Hinterland Law from the customary perspective, was the term and concept of "*adequate area* for farming and other enterprises *essential* to the necessities of the tribe" [emphases added] (GoL 2001, *article 66*). 'Adequate area' was also mentioned in Article 83 of the same law regarding the "Delimitation of tribal reserve" in the context of the need for a demarcation of an "adequate area for farming purposes of tribesmen before any land within the Territory of a Chiefdom shall be available for private purpose or grant of any kind whatever" (GoL 2001: 43). 'Adequate area' in both articles however was left undefined with regard to how such an area was to be determined, by whom, and what the 'essential' uses would be. The law did not include a 'definitions' section common to many laws in Anglophone countries. Nor did it refer to what a customary or tribal definition of 'adequate area' and 'essential' might be, how much land would be needed, and most importantly did not connect with local community or tribal boundaries that already existed. Not bringing the customary boundaries of chiefdoms already in existence into the definition of 'adequate area' or how this was to be determined, conflicted with customary concepts of 'early arrival', 'property constituting acts', and the inalienability of land, evidence,[10] and boundary demarcation. This set up a confused, aggrieved, and conflicted situation regarding the boundaries of tribes, ethnic groups, and lineages. It also allowed for the definitions of 'adequate area' and 'essential' to be played with, to the advantage of one or another parties involved or interested in the delimitation exercise. The outcome was (and continues to be) confusion about definitions, and how such areas were determined. There was also a good deal of ambiguity about what rights were and were not included in a concession. Particularly important in this regard was the confused understanding about the right to exclude others (local communities) from a government issued concession. Complicating the concept of 'adequate area', article 66 of the Hinterland Law stipulated that such an area also depended on "whether or not they [the tribes] have procured deeds from Government, delimiting by notes and bonds [likely meaning 'metes and bounds'] such reserves..." (GoL 2001, article 66: 37). However, how the possession of, or the procedure for obtaining such deeds was to intersect with 'adequate area' was not described, allowing further ambiguity into the overall problem. Additional ambiguity and confusion prevailed in locations with a mix of ethnic and religious populations. In these areas there existed ethnic and Muslim 'governors' who as local authorities appointed by and operating under the Ministry of the Interior, were empowered to adjudicate customary disputes for inhabitants of the same religious or ethnic group (also ICG 2006; GoL 2005). The fieldwork revealed that this was despite the existence of locally legitimate customary institutions and authorities engaged in the same tasks.

[10] Customary evidence in land disputes and claims includes, witnesses, elders called to indicate where a boundary is located, tombs and graves, trees, special landmarks such as specific rocks and other terrain features, which are then connected to 'stories' regarding the human-land interface over time. The stories are essentially the connection of history to parts of the physical landscape. The story must be tied in some way to the landscape to be useable customary evidence. So that if several people have the same story, connected to the same landscape, then that becomes powerful evidence in the customary domain.

Such ambiguity, while having utility to statutory officials to determine the status of specific areas using a wide variety of arguments, interests, and criteria, also resulted in deep and volatile animosity and tenure insecurity in the customary sector. As Bruce (2007) notes, a primary tension in statutory land law in Liberia is that there existed provisions protecting customary land rights, while different provisions facilitated the transfer of the same land to outsiders as public land. Whether such ambiguity was purposeful, for example in the derivation of the Hinterland Law, or its emergence inadvertent due to low capacity in legal drafting at the time, the outcome provided considerable 'room for maneuver' on the part of individuals knowledgeable and able to use the instruments of the state to pursue definitions in their favor, with no customary consultation. Such 'ambiguity as tool' was a frequent outcome of Liberian laws dealing with land and property, and resulted in significant grievance in the intersection of customary and formal law.

The emergence of ad hoc land and property norms

While the creation of the space for opportunism was one result of the tenurial confusion and ambiguity in Liberia, one of the more serious disruptive outcomes was the strong disincentive for rural native inhabitants to continue to participate in their own customary land laws that others (outsiders) were not following. While in other countries this can act to encourage customary inhabitants to use formal law, in Liberia this was not possible, leading to considerable instability in customary law. This contributed to the breakdown of customary laws and institutions regarding land, widening further the space for opportunism and driving the search for alternatives by rural inhabitants, particularly violence as a means to defend claims, resolve disputes, and acquire land. This search for alternatives led to the emergence of local, informal, *ad hoc* norms regarding aspects of land tenure. One example was the disillusionment of the rural youth with regard to the use of state sponsored customary law allowing chiefs to acquire and sell lineage customary land that otherwise would have gone to the youth. This disillusionment was pervasive, deeply aggrieved, and created an alternative 'legality' involving youth and violence.

A different *ad hoc* land and property norm that emerged from the interaction of customary, state sponsored customary, and formal law, had to do with a combination of 'woman damage', labor, and land. Land and marriage are intertwined in rural Liberia, and both were intensively controlled by customary elders (Richards 2005). To gain access to clan lands, a young man needed be in good standing with the elders who rule the descent group. There existed in the Hinterland Law (including the current revised version), two articles (article 54, Costs, fees, and Taxes; and article 55, Martial cases) which contained an array of fines for 'woman damage'[11] (GoL 2001). This aspect of state-sponsored customary law legally supported the derivation and maintenance of an *ad hoc* norm pursued by elders prior to the war, regarding purposefully seeking 'woman damage', and hence land and labor via the resulting fines. Richards (2005) describes this feature of rural life as a particularly important factor contributing to the war. Essentially the practice entailed the wife of an elder, being forced to 'call the name' of an accused male youth, thereby confessing to an extramarital affair. The accused male was then heavily fined and this converted to a labor obligation. The outcome was that those indebted were then unable to acquire land themselves and engage as a peer in customary life as they came of age. Apart from 'woman damage' many young men were heavily fined by elders for petty or other false charges and coerced to work off such fines with labor on the farms of elders, again preventing acquisition of land by younger men. This form of *ad hoc* norm became acutely exploitive prior to the war, and was used to accumulate land and labor for plantation development (also Davis 2007). This was perhaps one of the most problematic aspects of *ad hoc* land and property norms in Liberia, and set the youth against the male elders over issues of land and labor. Such land in-access by a younger generation that was intended to shunt them into labour and away from land also pushed them into militias (Richards 2005).[12]

Largely in response to the above, the re-emergence of the 'inalienability of land' as a customary legal concept manifested itself in Liberia by younger members of

[11] 'Woman damage' refers to extramarital relations, with the accused male being fined. The new inheritance law outlaws such damage seeking, thus constituting a contradiction with the Law Governing the Hinterland.

[12] Such an emergence of generational, land related *ad hoc* informal norms and groups connected to land and armed conflict is not isolated to Liberia. While present elsewhere in West Africa (Richards 2005) it is also present in Darfur, Sudan, with the emergence of the *Shabab,* an extreme pro-rebel youth group, which actively acts violently against their own elders for perceived transgressions. Among the top three conditions for the *Shabab* to be able to negotiate with the Sudanese government over an end to the conflict, expelling those whom have settled on land stolen from displaced farmers, is nearly as important as disarming government militias and prosecution for war crimes (Macfarquhar 2008).

lineages calling into question the 'right' of their elders or ancestors to have transferred land to outsiders, including sale, leasing, concessions, tribal deed issuance, etc. (Richards et al. 2004; Kuba and Lentz 2006). The fieldwork indicated that the *ad hoc* norm associated with this re-emergence, was that younger lineage members began to nullify such transfers themselves. This was strengthened by the increasingly popular norm that land transfer to outsiders was always revocable by the traditional landowning lineages (also ICG 2006). This is thus an example where the emergence of one *ad hoc* norm gave rise to another opposed norm.

Customary tenure versus statutory and state sanctioned customary law: tension and competition

(a) discriminatory pluralism

Significant animosity was generated in Liberia from a history of discriminatory land laws and policies in a pluralistic context. The first article of the Local Government Law drew a distinction between the 'county area' and the 'hinterland.' The county area included all land extending from the coast 40 miles inland, and 40 miles from the Mano and Cavalla rivers. The hinterland included the area beginning at the eastern boundary of the county area and extending to the national borders (GoL 1972, article 1; GoL 2001, article 1). This separation was important because different laws applied to the different areas. Such a purposeful form of spatial legal pluralism was important in the institutionalization of the separation between 'native' areas and the rest of the country. However this geographical distinction is arranged in formal law as the county area continually expanding against a contracting customary area, as land is acquired via the statutory tenure system, and in particular via state sponsored customary law. And while there was a requirement for obtaining the permission of indigenous authorities in order to proceed with land acquisition under fee simple, this was frequently not honored (Bruce 2007). Conversely however the research revealed that there was no mechanism other than violence for land to move back under customary control.

The Liberian Public Lands Law (GoL 1956, article 53) enshrined explicitly the division between those who were deemed 'civilized,' and those who were not, in a land tenure context. The law articulates the procedures for acquiring tribal lands in fee simple for those deemed 'civilized' in a separate article (GoL 1956, article 30) from that which applied to indigenous inhabitants once they became civilized (GoL 1956 article 53). As an indication of the discriminatory character of this divide, it was not only more difficult to obtain land in fee simple for 'civilized aborigines' than Americo-Liberians, but it was also more difficult for 'civilized aborigines' than it was for immigrants (GoL 1956, *articles 50, 51*). For Americo-Liberians there was no requirement for erecting a structure or bringing farmland under cultivation prior to receiving a deed in fee simple, as there was for immigrants and 'civilized aborigines,' nor was there a stated limit on the area of land that could be purchased (GoL 1956, articles 53, 30, 50, 51). Immigrants to Liberia could receive ten acres of farmland if single, or 25 acres if married. From this they needed to bring at least two acres under cultivation if farmland (type of crops unspecified), and if a town lot, needed to erect a house meeting specific conditions (GoL 1956, articles 50, 51). There were no requirements for immigrants to 'become civilized' prior to obtaining land in fee simple. Indigenous inhabitants however, were required to 'become civilized,' were only entitled to the same amount of land as immigrants, but with the added stipulation that at least a quarter of the land needed to be brought "under cultivation by planting coffee trees, palm trees, rubber, cocoa, or other trees or plants bearing marketable products" (GoL 1956, article 53). Thus compared to immigrants, more land needed to be brought under cultivation (2 out of 25 acres for married immigrants, vs. 6.25 out of a 25 acre allotment for married 'civilized aborigines'), but additionally for indigenous inhabitants the land needed to be planted in "marketable products" and preferably tree crops. The Hinterland Law further states that fines can be imposed on 'tribesmen' for not planting crops for market and for not taking such crops to market. To have both settlers and immigrants be advantaged over indigenous Liberians in terms of obtaining and using deeded land, engendered significant animosity among the latter, particularly given that all rural land to be obtained by these three categories of people, was initially indigenously held property.

Leasing land was an additional area of significant discrimination. Leasing (to foreigners) was provided for in the Public Lands Law, and could be pursued on public lands "not appropriated for other purposes" (GoL 1956, article 70). Here "appropriated for other purposes" indicates lands not already allocated in fee simple to another use, or used by the state, concessionaire, foreign mission or diplomatic post, or already leased by the state. As a result land customarily held was open to be leased via statutory law. Excluded from the article on leasing is the ability of customary individuals or communities to engage in direct leasing arrangements with foreign interests, or exercise a right of reversion subsequent to a lease. In the law, no reference is made as to what local communities might gain from such state appropriation of customary land for leasing, or any role of community permission for such appropriation.

A separate discriminatory issue was the way that the Local Government Law structured the administration of Counties and their subdivisions (Townships). 'Superintendents' were the highest ranking official of the counties and were appointed directly by the President, not elected or otherwise selected by the local population. Other locally elected county officials were subordinate to this position. The superintendent's duties included, among others, "investigate and settle, under the direction of the President, all difficulties between native tribes, and all matters appertaining to the aborigines not within the authority of the tribal chiefs" (GoL 1972, article 12). However The Rules and Regulations Governing Local Government Officials of the Political Sub-Divisions of Liberia, indicated that commissioners and superintendents were empowered to review all matters from the chiefdoms. As well, the corporate powers of each Township belonged to a presidentially appointed Commissioner. And the Commissioners "have the care of all public property in their respective townships" (GoL 1972, articles 80, 85). As well Townships as corporate bodies had the power to "take and hold real and personal property for the benefit of the township" (GoL 1972, articles 80, 85).

The Wildlife and National Parks Act (1987) further perpetuated the divisive, discriminatory approach to local communities and customary tenure. Two sections within Chapter 5 in particular were most problematic. Section 29, 'Establishment of Game Reserves and Controlled Hunting Areas', stipulated that the Wildlife Authority "may by regulation declare any area or land: (a) a Game Reserve for the protection, breeding and sustainable production of wildlife; (b) a Controlled Hunting Area in which hunting is controlled in accordance with regulations as may be issued by the Authority" (GoL 1987: 10). Thus Chapter 5 put in the hands of the Wildlife Authority the power to simply declare rural land to be no longer accessible to local communities who may already claim, reside in, or use an area. No consultation, pre-existing occupation, or compensation is mentioned. This is aggravated by Section 30, item 1 in the same Chapter, which states, "[n]o person shall hunt or capture any wild animal or enter into, settle, camp, cultivate, cut or burn trees or other vegetation or disturb wildlife in any way in a Game Reserve" (GoL 1987: 10). Clearly no settlements or farming were to be allowed in Game Reserves which were declared to exist by the Wildlife Authority. Again no mention is made of current occupants or claimants.

The Natural Resources Law, Chapter 6 'Ownership and Development of Mineral

Resources' (GoL 1999), describes opportunities for dispute resolution and other forms of redress. But these required literacy, significant financial resources, and knowledge of the formal legal system. While there was a list of the types of "[l]ands not subject to mining privileges" (article 146), the only customary land type listed are Poro (secret society) bush reserves, which are relatively small pieces of land. As well the article entitled, "Mining operation a public utility" (article 143) stipulated that because the mining industry is important to the development of the country, mining operations were considered a public utility and thus were justified in "the exercise of the power of eminent domain" (GoL 1999, 646). Thus like the Wildlife and National Parks Act, there was ample legal opportunity to obtain land already claimed by customary communities, with no consultation.

Concessions were a particular problem in Liberia. These were granted very freely prior to the war, but a great deal of land granted to concessions was never used. However local communities appear to have been nonetheless excluded from the entire concession area. Bruce (2007) describes an example where on one million acres granted in rubber concessions since 1926, less than 20 percent was ever developed.

(b) chiefs: selection, courts, trustees of communal holdings

Monrovia's control over the chieftain structure penetrated quite far into the functioning of customary life, including land tenure. While this control was variable, depending in-part on distance from Monrovia, a primary way this control was exercised was through selection of chiefs as an aspect of state sanctioned customary law. While the Local Government Law stipulated that chiefs (Paramount, Clan, and Town) were to be elected every four years, the Law Governing the Hinterland indicated that those who were able to participate in such elections was very narrowly defined. A Paramount Chief was to be elected only by the Council of Chiefs and Elders, and was subject to the approval of the President. A Clan Chief was to be elected only by members of the clan who were of legal age, and were owners of huts and not delinquent in their taxes. Town Chiefs were elected by the "paramount residents" of the village (GoL 2001, article 21). As well, in the case of death, resignation, or suspension of a chief, the Minister of Internal Affairs appointed an acting chief until an election was held (GoL 1972, Chap. 5, 22). Thus the laws were oriented toward a form of postcolonial indirect rule in which local chiefs did the state's work (via state sponsored customary law) by dealing with what were regarded as small, time-consuming tasks, including land cases. In return local chiefs received from the state broad powers within state sponsored customary law that allowed them to enrich themselves at the expense of local communities (ICG 2006; Richards 2005).

The connection between the state's involvement in selecting and supporting chiefs (and by implication influence in chief's courts), and the abuse of chiefly powers regarding land, labor, and marriage was significant. The government-created customary courts (under state sanctioned customary law) were administered by the Ministry of Internal Affairs. Thus Town Chiefs, Clan Chiefs, and Paramount Chiefs were responsible for original jurisdiction in customary law cases at different levels.[13] The fieldwork found that such customary courts were widely seen as corrupt and lacking in objectivity, legitimacy, and confidence among the customary sector. As a result land disputes frequently came to be resolved by violence but also by 'trial by ordeal'. In Liberia the latter usually occurred with the bark of the 'sassywood' tree made into a form of poison, with the accused either drinking it, or having it poured into the eyes, or the poison applied to a heated machete and put to the skin. If the person died, was blinded or injured, then s/he was guilty. Use of sassywood was seen as impartial. The use of trial by ordeal became common prior to the war due to the crippled formal and customary legal systems. While trial by ordeal is a form of customary law, it is also authorized as part of state sanctioned customary law as long as the life of the individual is not endangered (GoL 2001, article 73). Use of trial by ordeal in land cases was commonly as a form of appeal, after dissatisfaction with a decision made by a chief. And while the Liberian Supreme Court found trial by ordeal unconstitutional in 1949, the Rules Regulating the Hinterland (including its 2001 revision) continue to authorize it. The Ministry of Internal Affairs, in violation of both the judicial decision and the Constitution, did (and continues to) license 'ordeal doctors' to perform the rituals (GoL 2001, article 1; ICG 2006).

A further problem in the Hinterland Law, and an additional source of grievance and discrimination, was item b of article 66 which states that "this land interest

[13] Town Chiefs administered dispute resolution proceedings in towns, Clan Chiefs adjudicated between towns, and final decisions in Town Chief and Clan Chief courts would be appealed to the Paramount Chief courts (ICG 2006). Town and Clan Chiefs could also transfer complex cases that could not be resolved, to the Paramount Chief courts. Final judgments in Paramount Chief courts could be appealed to district commissioners and superintendents and finally to the Ministry's Office of Tribal Affairs in Monrovia.

[regarding adequate area] may be transmitted into communal holdings upon application of a tribe made to the government for that purpose"; and item c (same article) indicating that the "communal holding will be vested in the Paramount Chief and Tribal Authority as Trustees for the tribe" (GoL 2001, article 66: 37). The fieldwork found that these two items together created a significant tension between indigenous customary law and state sponsored customary land law. For land to be deeded as a communal holding it needed to be surveyed, with the survey attached to the 'adequate area' term, concept, and delimitation. There was (and is) considerable reluctance for customary community members to move forward with a communal deed application if they did not agree with the state as to the boundaries or quantity of land to be included, because such a deed would only support the state's definition and delimitation of 'adequate area'. On the other hand there was considerable willingness on the part of the Paramount Chief and 'Tribal Authority' to have an 'adequate area' transmitted to such communal holdings, because they were the trustees that the holding was then vested in. It was noted a number of times in the fieldwork that the descendents of such trustees had acted to have such communal land deeded entirely to them as individuals, based on the fact that their father's name was on the communal land document, followed by "et al." This latter arrangement was another *ad hoc* land and property norm that contributed to the volatile situation between state sponsored and indigenous customary law. This also fed the notion among younger rural inhabitants that the earlier transmission of land to 'communal holdings' was not legitimate, and needed to be revoked, with such revocation itself emerging as an *ad hoc* land and property norm. This is thus another example where one *ad hoc* norm contributed to the derivation of another, opposed, grievance based, norm.

By the state making it lucrative for the chief (and associated elders) to engage in activities via state sponsored customary law that were opposed to the desires of local community members, a volatile tension was produced in which very different interests in land tenure were pursued by the leadership versus the wider community. There was little recourse against the chief or other elders with regard to abuses and exercise of prerogatives, outside of violence.

Conclusion

The end to the war in Liberia has not brought an end to the volatile nature of the socio-legal space regarding land tenure in the country. Deep animosities and tensions over land have not been resolved by the signing of the peace accord, nor by the large military and civil affairs presence of UMNIL (United Nations Mission in Liberia), and the various donors present in the country (Unruh 2009). The land tenure problems in the country are still acute. Disputes over land are the "most explosive issue in Liberia today" (CGAR 2009: 8). The President of the country has "expressed fear that the issue of land reform, if not swiftly redressed by the government and its international partners, could crop up into another war in the country" (Daygbor 2007); and the Crisis Group Africa Report echoes this, indicating that land disputes could be a root cause of any subsequent insurgency (CGAR 2009). Land rights-related violence has continued to occur or has increased in different parts of the country (NC 2007; GOL 2006; Unruh 2009; CGAR 2009), and in some areas, progress achieved by UNMIL to enforce formal land laws, has been scuttled as people return to the illegal extraction of rubber, timber, and diamonds, as well as squatting and forced eviction. And Richards (2005: 587) indicates that, "[y]oung people without secure tenancy rights will continue to float in the countryside without stable social commitments, and thus remain vulnerable to both chiefs and militia recruiters" (also Corriveau-Bourque 2007). The administrative and judicial systems required to handle land matters in the postwar context, while initially underdeveloped, nonfunctional and overstretched, are improving, particularly with regard to the work of the Governance Reform Commission, which has recently established a Land Commission. However there is a profound lack of trained personnel to manage the property rights system and to adjudicate disputes (GRC 2007). As a result, presently between 75 and 90 percent of all cases in all statutory courts (probate, civil, criminal, appellate) are land and property related (Unruh 2009; GRC 2007).

What is needed in postwar Liberia is an appreciation of the historical and structural process by which land tenure in the country became increasingly aggravated and explosive. This is important because addressing land tenure in the postwar period will require more than simply a rework of statutory laws. It will in addition require a reformulation of the socio-legal relationship between statutory law, customary law and society that takes into account, 1) a needed corrective to the abuse by the urban elite and customary leadership that emerged from the interaction of state sponsored customary law with other sets of laws and norms, 2) the ongoing robust presence of *ad hoc* land and property norms which continue to take on new directions, 3) a much needed rework of the statutory legal environment that de-emphasizes 'integrity of the law' and places more emphasis on 'law and society', 4) a reinstatement of the *Liberian Law Journal* and greater priority given to customary law as a topic of examination, analysis, and legal recommendation, and 5) the derivation and institution of a form of 'customary law officer' similar to what exists in neighboring Sierra Leone, able to act as an interface between statutory and customary law.

The Liberia case is instructive in that it provides a setting to examine the socio-legal interactions involving land rights which can be a significant contributor to civil wars. In Liberia the interaction within the tenurial socio-legal space involved sets of land-related laws and norms that became set against one another over time in a mutually aggravating way. The roots of the problem are embedded in the country's history, legal capacity, and different forms of logic regarding rights to land, together with an emphasis placed on the non-interaction of these forms of logic. With no legitimate institution or authority able to resolve the resulting acute tensions, for many there appeared to be little opportunity for recourse to perceived prolonged injustice, other than violence.

References

ALLOTT, A.
1967 'A Report on the feasibility of research into Liberian customary law.' *Liberian Law Journal* 3: 83-100.

ANDRE, C.
2003 'Custom, contracts and cadastres in north-west Rwanda.' in T.A Benjaminsen and C. Lund (eds.), *Securing Land Rights in Africa*. London: CASS Publishing.

BANKS, P.
2007 'Issues paper on reforming Liberia's legal and judicial system towards enhancing the rule of law.' Governance Reform Commission, Monrovia: Republic of Liberia.

BLACK, H.
1991 *Black's Law Dictionary,* St. Paul, MN, USA, West Publishing Co.

BROPLEH, N.D.
1989 'Land tenure and land use policies. green revolution action plan, phase 1: 1990-1992, background support paper no. 1. Monrovia: Food and Agriculture Organization of the United Nations.

BRUCE, J.W. and S.E. MIGOT-ADHOLLA
1994 *Searching for Land Tenure Security in Africa*. Dubuque, Iowa: The World Bank and Kendall/Hunt Publishing Co.

BRUCE, J.W.
2007 'Insecurity of land tenure, land law and land registration in Liberia: a preliminary assessment.' Washington DC: The World Bank.

CHABAL, P., DALOZ, J.
1999 *Africa Works: Disorder as Political Instrument*. Bloomington IN, USA: Indiana University Press.

CORRIVEAU-BOURQUE, A.
2007 'An environment for recruitment: power and marginalization in Liberia.' Montreal: McGill University Program for International Development Studies, Honors Thesis.

CGAR (Crisis Group Africa Report).
2009 'Liberia: uneven progress in security sector reform.' *Crisis Group Africa Report* No. 148, 13 January.

CEUPPENS, B.
2006 'Allochthons, colonizers, and scroungers: exclusionary populism in Belgium.' *African Studies Review* 49: 147-186.

DAVIS, J.
2007 'Tree crop sub sector report.' Liberia Agriculture Sector Review, Monrovia and Washington DC: World Bank.

DAYGBOR, J.
2007 'Land dispute - country's next war trigger.' *The Analyst,* Monrovia AllAfrica Global Media. Monrovia, 21 March.

DELVILLE, P.L.
2003 'When farmers use 'pieces of paper' to record their land transactions in francophone rural Africa: insights into the dynamics of institutional innovation.' in T.A. Benjaminsen and C. Lund (eds.), *Securing Land Rights in Africa*, London: CASS Publishing.

EBOH, S.O.
2005 *Inalienability of Land and Citizenship in the African Context* Frankfurt: IKO-Verlag fur Interkulturelle Kommunikation.

ENGERMAN, S.L.
2004 *Land Rights, Ethno-nationality, and Sovereignty in History*. London: Routledge.

FAY, D.
2009 'Property, subjection and protected areas: the 'restitution' of Dwesa-Cwebe Nature Reserve, South Africa.' in D. Fay and D. James (eds.) *The Rights and Wrongs of Land Restitution: 'Restoring What Was Ours*. New York: Routledge-Cavendish.

GESCHIERE, P. and S. JACKSON
2006 'Autochthony and the crisis of citizenship: democratization, decentralization, and the politics of belonging.' *African Studies Review* 49: 1-8.

GRC (Governance Reform Commission)
2007 The way forward: land & property right issues in the republic of Liberia.' Governance Reform Commission, Monrovia: Government of Liberia'

GoL (Government of Liberia).
1956 *Liberian Public Lands Law*, Monrovia: Vol III. Government of Liberia.
1972 *Local Government Law*, Monrovia: Government of Liberia.
1986 *Right to Own Property. Article 22*, Constitution of the Republic of Liberia: Monrovia: Government of Liberia.
1987 *Wildlife and National Parks Act*. Game reserves, controlled hunting areas and other protected areas, Chapter *V*. Monrovia: Government of Liberia.
1999 *Natural Resources Law*. Ownership and development of mineral resources. *Liberian Codes Revised*, *Vol IV*, Monrovia, Government of Liberia.
2001 *Revised Laws and Administrative Regulations for Governing the Hinterland, Ministry of the Interior*, Monrovia: Government of Liberia.
2005 *Rules and Regulations Governing Local Government Officials of the Political Sub-Divisions of Liberia, Revised Edition*, Ministry of Internal Affairs, Monrovia, Government of Liberia, 24 February,.
2006 *Liberia Statement of Policy Intent for Agriculture*. Ministry of Agriculture, Monrovia: Government of Liberia,

GRIFFITHS, J.
1986 'What is Legal Pluralism?' *Journal of Legal Pluralism* 24 :1-52.

HERB, G.H., KAPLAN, D.H.
1999 *Nested Identities: Nationalism, Territory, and Scale*. Boulder: Rowman and Littlefield Publishers.

HOHE, T.
2005 'Developing local governance.' in G Junne and W Verkoren (eds.), *Postconflict Development: Meeting New Challenges,* Boulder: Lynne Rienner.

ICG (International Crisis Group)
2006 'Liberia: restructuring the justice system.' *International Crisis Group Africa Report,* Brussels No. 107.
2004 'Liberia and Sierra Leone: rebuilding failed states.' *International Crisis Group Africa Report,* Brussels No. 87.

IRIN
2007 *Liberia: Donor Fatigue Threatening DDR Process*. UN Office for the Coordination of Humanitarian Affairs.

JACKSON, S.
2006 'Sons of which soil? the language and politics of autochthony in eastern DR Congo.' *African Studies Review* 49: 95-124.

KOLLIE, J.
2006 'Report of the situation of land tenure in Liberia.' Rome: Food and Agriculture Organization of the UN.

KUBA, R. and C. LENTZ, C. (eds.)
2006 *Land and the Politics of Belonging in West Africa*. Boston: Brill Press.

LANDAU, L.B.
2006 'Transplants and Transients: Idioms of Belonging and in Innercity Johannesburg.' *African Studies Review* 49: 125-146.

LEYNSEELE, von Y. and P. HEBINCK
2009 'Through the prism: the reworking of land resititution settlements in South Africa.' in D. Fay and D. James (eds.) *The Rights and Wrongs of Land Restitution: Restoring What Was Ours,* New York: Routledge-Cavendish.

MCCARTHY, N.
2007 *Customary Land Use in Liberia: A Review of Supreme Court Decisions*. Monrovia: IFPRI and George Mason University School of Law.

MAGANGA, F.
2003 'The interplay between formal and informal systems of managing resource conflicts: some evidence from south-western Tanzania.' in T. A. Benjaminsen and C. Lund, C. (eds.), *Securing Land Rights in Africa*, London: CASS Publishing.

MACFARQUHAR, N.
2008 'The scared sheiks.' *The New York Times*, December 21.

MARSHALL-FRATANI, R.
2006 'The war of "who is who": autochthony, nationalism, and citizenship in the Ivorian crisis.' *African Studies Review* 49: 9-44.

MCAUSLAN, P.
1998 'Making law work: restructuring land relations in Africa.' *Development and Change* 29: 529-552.
2003 *Bringing The Law Back In: Essays in Land Law and Development*. Burlington: Ashgtate Publishing Limited.

MERRY, S.
1988 'Legal pluralism.' *Law and Society Review* 22: 869-896.

MOORE, S.
1973 'Law and social change: the semi-autonomous social field as an appropriate field of study.' *Law and Society Review* 7: 719.
NC (National Chronicle)
2007 'In Firestone shooting: two security personnel wounded.' *National Chronicle*, February 19, Monrovia.
OKOTH-OGENDO, H.W.O.
2000 'Legislative approaches to customary tenure and tenure reform in East Africa.' Pp. 123-134 in T. Toulmin and J. Quan (eds.) *Evolving Land Rights, Policy and Tenure in Africa*. London: Natural Resources Institute.
PLATTEAU, J.P.
2000 'Does Africa need land reform?' Pp. 51-74 in T. Toulmin and J. Quan (eds.), *Evolving Land Rights, Policy and Tenure in Africa*. London: Natural Resources Institute.
PLUMMER, B.
2007 'Land tenure: the neglected path to social security and reconstruction in Liberia Montreal: McGill University Program for International Development Studies, Honors Thesis.
PLUNKETT, M.
2005 'Reestablishing the rule of law.' in G. Junne and W. Verkoren (eds.), *Postconflict Development: Meeting New Challenges*, Boulder: Lynne Rienner.
RICHARDS, P.
2005 'To fight or to farm? agrarian dimensions of the Mano River Conflicts Liberia and Sierra Leone.' *African Affairs* 104: 571-590.
RICHARDS, P., S. ARCHIBALD, B. BRUCE, W. MODAD, E. MULBAH, T. VARPILAH and J. VINCENT
2004 'Community cohesion in Liberia: a post-conflict rapid social assessment. Monrovia: African Knowledge Associates.
RIDDELL, J. and C. DICKERMAN
1986 'Land tenure profile: Liberia.' in J. Riddell, and C. Dickerman (eds.), *Country Profiles of Land Tenure: Africa 1986*. Madison, WI: Land Tenure Center, University of Wisconsin, Madison.
RUSSELL, W.B.
1997 *People and the Land through Time: Linking Ecology and History*. New Haven: Yale University Press.
SAWYER, A.
2005 *Beyond Plunder: Toward Democratic Governance in Liberia*. London: Lynne Rienner Publishers.

TOULMIN, C. and J. QUAN, J.

2000 *Evolving Land Rights, Policy and Tenure in Africa*. London: Natural Resources Institute.

UNEP (United Nations Environment Programme)

2004 *Desk Study on the Environment in Liberia*. Nairobi: UN Environmental Programme.

UNRUH, J.

2002 'Poverty and property rights in the developing world: not as simple as we would like.' *Land Use Policy* 19: 275-276.

2009 'Land rights in postwar Liberia: the volatile part of the peace process.' *Land Use Policy* 26: 425-433.

WILY, L.

2007 *So Who Owns the Forest: an Investigation into Forest Ownership and Customary Land Rights in Liberia*. Brussels: Sustainable Development Institute/FERN.

WORLD BANK

2007 Concept note Liberia: the role of land tenure in confronting the challenges of transition – a strategic plan for accelerating growth and investment in the urban and rural sectors. Washington, DC: World Bank.

THE STRUGGLE FOR CONTEXT IN THE PROTECTION OF CHILDREN'S RIGHTS: UNDERSTANDING THE CORE CONCEPTS OF THE AFRICAN CHILDREN'S CHARTER

Thoko Kaime

Introduction

Many African children have to negotiate different social spaces adapting to various roles to suit their situation. Consequently, any proposed framework for the promotion and protection of their rights must be flexible enough to take into account and be of relevance to the specific circumstances of each particular child. In this regard, Africa's pre-eminent document on children's rights, the *African Charter on the Rights and Welfare of the Child* (the 'African Children's Charter', 'the Charter') must propound principles that are general enough to address the multiple configurations of meaning and perspectives that are and inform children's rights and which emerge from the contexts in which children live.

Although the rights and duties in the African Children's Charter cover almost every aspect of the child's life, there are four cross-cutting principles that may be thought of as underpinning the entire instrument. These include the rule against discrimination (African Children's Charter 1990: art. (3)), the 'best interests' rule (African Children's Charter 1990: art. 4), the rule promoting the child's survival and development (African Children's Charter 1990: art. 5), and the rule requiring the child's participation (African Children's Charter 1990: arts. 4(2) & 7). The

African Children's Committee has also identified these principles as constituting the central focus of the rights and duties contained in the Charter and of the reporting system under it (African Children's Committee n.d. The African Children's Charter 1990: art 43(1) requires every state party to submit to the Committee reports on the measures that they have adopted which give effect to the Charter. Cf UN Committee on the Rights of the Child 2003: para. 12). The Committee, therefore, requires that relevant information, including the principal legislative, judicial and administrative or other measures in force or foreseen, should be provided in respect of the general principles (African Children's Committee n.d.: para. 11). In addition, states parties are advised to provide relevant information on the impact and application of these principles in relation to the implementation of the other provisions of the Charter (African Children's Committee n.d.: para. 12). However, the relevance of the general principles transcends their application to the state reporting mechanism. Given their generality and extensive scope, they apply to all considerations relating to the promotion and protection of the rights and welfare of the child and, therefore, serve as an ideal starting point for any analysis of the substantive provisions of the Charter as well as the situation of children in different contexts.

Since the core concepts of the African Children's Charter are derivative concepts, inquiries into their development, meaning and scope are more or less settled. There will, therefore, be much less contestation with regard to the meaning, scope and applicability of these principles. However, the case is different when it comes to the operation of these principles at the local level. In this regard, universal norms must be tempered with and operate within the parameters of local observation and custom (Hellum 1999: 71-79).

The General Principles and Cultural Context: The Basis for an Ethnographic Approach

By taking into account the specificities of children's lives, this analysis reinforces the perspective on the relationship between culture, children's rights and law, and therefore cements an approach to children's rights that avoids the age old dichotomies between human rights universals and cultural absolutes. Instead, we must focus on the multiple configurations of meaning representing "a network of perspectives" (Hannerz 1992: 11) that emerges from the situated contexts in which children and their guardians live. This type of analysis allows us not only to investigate how the general principles of the Charter have manifested themselves but also to go further and see how these basic principles structure and effect power relations between children and their guardians.

However, a grounded approach to the implications and relevance of the general principles raises difficult methodological problems. Such constraints arise in part because of the model of law that informs law at the national as well as international level (A. Griffiths 2001: 103). This model is one which promotes a uniform view of law and its relationship to the state and citizens (J. Griffiths 1986: 3). It establishes boundaries between the legal and social domains and the rules associated with them. These domains exist in a hierarchical relationship so that the legal rules are not only set apart from, but acquire greater authority and precedence over social rules (Roberts 1979: 29) and are used to determine outcomes when conflict arises (Comaroff and Roberts 1981: 5). Consequently, the law is removed from the domain of social life and posited as an autonomous field with immunity from the kind of considerations that permeate every day existence (A. Griffiths 2001: 104).

In reality, however, life offers a multiplicity of legal orders (Tamanaha 1995). Thus, explicitly announced legal rules such as the general principles of the African Children's Charter are not the only vehicles of normativity; these legislative artefacts complement a variety of indigenous and customary rules and practices through which they find expression. Viewed in this manner, it is clear that the general principles may be viewed not as law *simpliciter*, but also as a species of cultural practice. Describing children's rights as cultural practice calls for a view of children's rights as an essentially porous multi-polar regime constituting an array of intersections where distinct processes crisscross and are coloured by cultural context.

In order to achieve this rendering of children's rights, it is important to formulate a dialogue that is capable of accommodating the diversity of children's situations whilst at the same time emphasising their shared experiences. Whilst elucidating the meaning and scope of the core principles of the African Children's Charter is an appropriate starting point, the process needs to be complemented with a form of knowledge that goes beyond abstract propositions that are constitutive of children's rights norms at international law, a form of knowledge that is grounded in the specific contexts of children's lives. To acquire such knowledge, concrete data from the lived reality of children's situations is required. Such endeavours afford a grounded approach to the promotion and protection of the rights and welfare of the child.

Taking account of this, the following analysis of the African Children's Charter departs from orthodox legal analysis and attempts to present a picture of the general principles in action in the lives of the children and adults of Magombo and Ndalama village where I conducted fieldwork between July 2004 and May 2005. The two villages are located in Thyolo District in southern Malawi and the majority of their inhabitants belong to the Lomwe tribe. In total, I held one-to-one interviews with 47 children and 56 adults. Of the 47 children, 32 were boys; and of the 56 adults, 41 were women. 35 of the children were in the age range between 11 and 18 whilst the rest were between six and 10. Further to that, I recorded 11 conversations with families which I defined for my notes as group conversations with either a mother and a father or each one of these or both and a child or children. I also maintained two focus groups at Thyolo Secondary School and Mpinji Community Day Secondary School with eight and 11 participants respectively. I recorded eight sessions with each of the focus groups. It cannot be claimed that the picture presented is comprehensive but nonetheless it does raise significant issues that inform discourse when it is brought from the 'global to the local.'

Non-Discrimination: Concepts, Context and Contests

The African Children's Charter purports to extend all the rights set forth in the instrument to each individual child. It stipulates that:

> Every child shall be entitled to the enjoyment of the rights and freedoms recognised and guaranteed in this Charter irrespective of the child's or his or her parents' or legal guardians race, ethnic group, colour, sex, language, relation, political or other opinion, national or social origin, fortune, birth or other status (African Children's Charter 1992: art. 3).

Article 3 applies to *every* child and is applicable with reference to *all* the rights and freedoms guaranteed by the African Children's Charter. In other words, it is a non-autonomous provision of the Charter (Bayefsky 1990: 3-4). It has no independent existence, yet it qualifies all of the other substantive provisions of the Charter as if it were a part of each one. Thus, it governs all of the rights and freedoms recognised and guaranteed in the Charter, hence its status as a general principle.

However, although it is relatively easy to delineate the meaning and scope of the non-discrimination clause of the Charter, conceptualising child discrimination within Lomwe social space is not an easy task. This is because the cultural construction of the child is synonymous with the idea of *mphatso* or gift. According to Lomwe cosmology, *mphatso* must be treated with the utmost care and should not be abused lest the spirit of the giver is offended and causes ruin. In the case of the child, the giver is no less than *chisumphi* or God himself. All Lomwe know that when *chisumphi* is not pleased, his anger has devastating consequences. Consequently, no parent or guardian would own up to treating any child under his or her care in a discriminatory fashion.

The situation is compounded even more because the word that expresses discrimination amongst the Lomwe is *kusankha*. Used in this context, it always carries a negative connotation. Thus, according to Lomwe custom *kusankha* of any type is wrong. According to Village head Ndalama, any one who perpetrates *kusankha*, whether at home or at the work place, is essentially provoking the displeasure of the spirits. *Kusankha* is, therefore, roundly condemned within Lomwe cultural space. Consequently, in order to investigate more thoroughly the conception and incidence of discrimination as it relates to children, it is important to adopt terms of discourse that do not put the matter beyond discussion as is the case with the concept of *kusankha*. It is in view of this that different terminology was used in order to fully investigate the conception and incidence of discrimination. The term that was adopted is *kusiyanitsa*. The English equivalent of *kusiyanitsa* is differentiation. Although used in the context of discrimination, it is less value-laden than *kusankha* and, therefore, does not immediately invite a reproachful finger. *Kusiyanitsa* may sometimes be justified, and often is, and therefore does not convey the negative connotations associated with *kusankha*. Thus, after encountering the almost unanimous opinion regarding *kusankha* and the limited possibilities it presented during the early stages of the fieldwork, I subsequently employed the concept of *kusiyanitsa* to inquire into various aspects relating to discrimination in the context of children.

However, although *kusankha* is described as culturally unacceptable, it does not mean that discrimination against children is non-existent. My conversations with different children as well as parents and guardians revealed the existence of discriminatory practices on various grounds. For example, participants pointed out instances of discrimination predicated on the grounds of poverty, disability, age, sex and gender. Amongst all these, the most identified ground was discrimination on the ground of sex and gender. However, regardless of the nature or basis of the discrimination, it is clear that its impact on children is significant.

There were other cases where boys and girls were turned away from school because their parents could not afford to buy uniforms for them even though I was informed that the government had issued a directive instructing teachers not to turn back students due to inability to purchase a uniform. In all these cases, there was a consensus that the lack of economic capacity should not have been used as a ground for *kusiyanitsa*.

Whereas discrimination within institutional settings such as school or the local hospital is easily identifiable and relatively easy to tackle, such is not the case with discrimination that takes place within the family. This is because a child's questioning of discriminatory practices is labelled as insubordination and may lead to curtailment of other avenues of support. In this context, the most prevalent example of discrimination reveals itself in the form of practices that encourage the practice of son-preference and the subordination of girl-children. Son-preference is a form of sex or gender based discrimination that reveals itself through a host of socio-cultural and religious attitudes perpetuating the supposed superiority of the male child whilst consigning his sisters to disadvantage. For example, when Mercy Kanama and her brother, from Ndalama village, were selected to pursue secondary education at Mpinji Community Day Secondary School in Ndalama village, it presented a financial problem to their father. The father subsequently resolved the situation by paying school fees for Mercy's brother and ordering Mercy to drop out of school. The following year another brother was selected to a different secondary school outside Ndalama village and her father was able to put money together for his school fees. When I asked Mercy's mother about the *kusiyanitsa* between Mercy and her brothers, she said:

> We are all brought up differently. Sometimes it's just that the person is not kind hearted.... But it is also true that some people believe that girl-children will not be helpful in future. So, to them, I say to them, it makes sense not to spend money on their daughters.

It is instructive that during our conversation, reference to Mercy's father was sanitised and relegated to an allusion to *munthuyo* or *anthu ena*: 'the person' or 'some people', terms which are befitting of references to strangers. It is this aspect of intra-family alienation that makes it difficult to tackle *kusiyanitsa* within the family. The wrongs of family members holding power are 'othered' in a way that not only limits avenues for redress but provides a fertile environment for sustaining a discriminatory attitude.

Thus, it is clear that, despite an underlying belief that *kusankha* or discrimination is essentially inconsistent with Lomwe cultural practices and beliefs, there still persist practices that go against this sanction. It is, therefore, crucial to go beyond the conception of discrimination and unpack the socio-cultural basis of the practices and discover why they still occur. In this regard, it is important to point out there are two opposing viewpoints that inform attitudes relating to discriminatory practices relating to children. On one hand, there are arguments to the effect that some forms of *kusiyanitsa* are acceptable whilst on the other, there is the view that any form of *kusiyanitsa* that results in unfairness is unacceptable. Although the former view had comparatively fewer proponents than the latter, its existence justifies serious consideration. Consequently, in the subsequent two sections, I examine the issue of *kusiyanitsa* along these two paradigms.

Maybe not good but justifiable: Analysing the pro-distinction narratives

As has been explained, *kusankha* automatically has negative connotations. Consequently, instances of discriminatory practice veiled as mere *kusiyanitsa* usually carry with them some form of justification. One of the most common justificatory explanations was economic incapacity. In this regard, it is suggested that, when parents or guardians find themselves in difficult economic circumstances, they are sometimes forced to make choices that may adversely affect the rights and welfare of some of the children under their care. The intention is not to treat the children differently but it is said that the situation merely forces their hand. A conversation I had with John Mthawira, a tyre smith at Thyolo District Market, highlights this type of justification. He explained how his eldest child, Timothy, dropped out of school and ended up working with him at the tyre repair stall whilst his younger son, Tamando, continued with schooling:

> When Tamando was selected to go to secondary school, his brother had just finished his Form Two[1] and was supposed to start the next class. I could not afford to pay fees for the both of them. I, therefore, decided that since Timothy had already accomplished

[1] Form Two is the second year of secondary school and the tenth year of a child's progressive education.

> a bit of secondary education, his brother should also have a taste.

While there is some tragic logic to cases like that of the Mthawiras, this must be contrasted with cases like Mercy Kanama's situation. It is revealing that her father was able to put together funds for her younger brother a year after she had been selected to go to secondary school, yet he would not do the same for her. Thus, in the case of other vulnerable children such as orphans or girl-children, the choice may be more economic than appears at first sight. In the past, an orphaned child was welcomed because it guaranteed steady labour within the household and economic security in old age. However, changes in the modes of production from subsistence farming to a cash-based economy as well as the general mobility of rural populations has put a strain on the children's duty to help parents. Whereas many elders stress this duty, it is becoming more widely recognised that its conceptualisation is changing from that of a duty to that of mere goodwill. Consequently, care for orphans, and in some cases, girl-children is considered by some parents and guardians as a thankless task without any discernible benefit. Mai Nahipa, a community social worker who runs children's rights awareness courses and as well manages an orphanage in Ndalama village, explained the incidence of orphans in Magombo and Ndalama village in the following terms:

> Ten years ago... maybe fifteen years ago, there were no orphans in this village. It does not mean that parents were not dying. They were dying. However, taking on the responsibility for such children brought you honour and maybe wealth later on.... Nowadays, if you start bothering with orphans, it just brings you poverty so people see no point in it. Even when the children are their brother's or sister's. All the children that you see here, perhaps except for one or two, have got uncles, aunts and grandparents in this village. But did they take them?

Village head Magombo shares similar sentiments. He points out that under Lomwe custom there is a general duty to help out your kin when they have problems. However, he seems to endorse the poverty plea when he rhetorically asks: 'How can you enjoy sugarcane when you have no teeth?'

Another ground for *kusiyanitsa* is the sanitisation of difference and with it the normalisation of practices that perpetuate unjustifiable *kusiyanitsa*. A consideration of a series of folk sayings or proverbs reveals this aspect. For example, proverbs such as *mwana wa mwini n'gaga, saundika* [Your friend's or neighbour's child is like *nsima*[2]of maize husks, it cannot be moulded]; *kwa eni kulibe mkuwe, mutu wa nkhuku n'chiwalo* [When amongst strangers one does not shout, the head of a chicken is a proper chicken piece]; *ukadya kumadziwa kuti azungu ndi alendo* [While you are eating remember that Europeans are strangers]; and *mbalame ya kwao siiwala* [a bird with a home does not forget such home] indicate that *kusiyanitsa* towards others who are not members of your immediate family is tolerable. Although this sort of attitude stands in stark contrast with the *kuthandizana* or 'help thy neighbour' ethos that is claimed to permeate Lomwe society, it is a candid reminder of the socio-economic changes that have upturned the values and priorities within families.

Furthermore, some elements of Lomwe cosmology also seem to approbate discriminatory actions against children. Lomwe people believe that the universe is finally balanced, and that for any act of goodwill the benefactor will later enjoy a return favour. The antithesis of this belief is also held to be true and is expressed in the proverb *choyipa chitsata mwini* [Evil follows the wrongdoer]. However, the problem with the operation of this concept is that it may not be the perpetrator him- or herself who pays the tariff but even other members of his family including children. Although only two individuals expressed views connecting child discrimination and the inevitable operation of the Fates, the belief in the proposition that *choyipa chitsata mwini* is significant with 56% of all adults and 36% of all children interviewed expressing belief in it.

Whereas poverty and supernatural intervention have been advanced as explanations for various instances of differential treatment of children, the most identified justification and also the basis for the most pervasive type of discrimination, is difference. Although belief in the logic of difference holds sway amongst many older parents and guardians, the belief is not absent amongst younger parents either. One of the latter, Mai Anne Wyson from Magombo village, points out why differential treatment occurs:

> Boys are stronger and most of the times they are more intelligent and help their parents more than the girls.... If you asked any woman in this village, they would say they prefer to have a son. Sons help more.

---

[2]*Nsima* is the daily food of the majority of Malawians. It is made from maize flour whose husks have been removed.

Mr Davison Wyson concurs with his wife. However, his explanation is more philosophical. He argues that *chisumphi* or god made man stronger because he is the one with the duty to look after the family. Parents must, therefore, ensure that boy-children grow up to take up this responsibility. This, he points out, is something no one who is in his right frame of mind can argue against. Consequently, acting to change the way things are entails going against the logic of difference. Such endeavours are not always well received. Mai Malindira frowns upon efforts that seek to renegotiate the position of women and girl-children within the family home. She reckons that such activities only serve to disturb family harmony and bring confusion:

> We just look at all these women running about, talking about 'jenda'.[3] Yet, when their husbands beat them like *tchopa*[4] drum, they run to *ankhoswe*.[5] If our way of life was so bad, why then go to the *ankhoswe*?
>
> ...If the women of this village stuck to looking after their husbands as they ought to, and minding the kitchen as a good woman should; then their husbands wouldn't be spending their money at the beer hall at the Boma and on the prostitutes in Ndalama village.

The benefits of keeping to one's position within the family are, therefore, obvious and submission to patriarchy is equated with good behaviour. Yet, whether the basis of the discriminatory act lies in the poverty of money or the poverty of the mind, the very fact of it taking place reveals a belief that one particular child is worth less than another; that that particular child is not deserving of equal concern.[6] It is a kind of conviction that is difficult to reconcile with the Lomwe conception of children and childhood. However, this is not an attitude that is without challenge. Many parents, guardians and children believe that any form of

[3] *Jenda* is the vernacularised equivalent of gender equality and women's rights but it is also used in some contexts to refer to human rights generally.

[4] *Tchopa* is a type of dance much loved by the Lomwe.

[5] *Ankhoswe* are traditional marriage counsellors.

[6] Compare the views of Langa DCJ in *Bhe v Magistrate, Khayelitsha and others*, CCT 49/03 (South Africa) paras 54-59.

kusiyanitsa that is based on unfairness is inherently wrong and, far from being a reflection of Lomwe culture and custom, it is in fact evidence of its breakdown. In the following section, I briefly outline the basis and strength of views supportive of non-discrimination.

It is not part of our culture: An inquiry into non-discrimination discourse

One notable aspect relating to narratives that support non-discrimination perspectives is that they are not only based on children's rights discourse but also on an eclectic mix of cultural, religious and spiritual arguments. Consequently, non-discrimination perspectives are not the preserve of '*ajenda*' or human rights advocates alone but also that of ordinary people who claim no special knowledge of children's rights.

One such ordinary person is Mai Nkhululu who lives in Magombo village. Mai Nkhululu is in her late forties and has four children, the youngest of whom is seventeen years old. Recalling her experience as to the manner in which she brought up her daughter and three sons, she says:

> One really does not have a choice as to the kind of children one will have. God gives you a son, you say thank you. You also say thank you if he gives you a daughter....
>
> ...[O]ur culture says that children are gifts. Boys and girls, all are gifts. That is how it is. So you care for them in the same way. Whether it is food, clothes or chores around the house.

The equal treatment of children that Mai Nkhululu refers to is at the core of attitudes that do not condone child discrimination. Such a perspective is very much interconnected with the conception of children as gifts. It is a logical extension to a cultural worldview that posits children as special and worthy of equal protection and affection. Mai Nkhululu's views are shared by her neighbour, Mai Sambalikagwa. She argues that subjecting children to discriminatory practice is inherently wrong because it amounts to cruelty [*nkhanza*] and any cruelty goes against the fundamentals of Lomwe culture and the requirements of good parenting.

Pragmatism is another reason that sustains non-discrimination perspectives. For example, in families where all the children are of the same sex, it is difficult to sustain gendered roles in the allocation of family responsibilities. In these families, the allocation of resources and affection does not follow the patriarchal patterns that serve to promote son-preference. One of my key participants, Yaya,[7] who always insisted that I bring a bottle of Fanta for our conversations (on the grounds that my endless questions 'stole' her voice), had the 'misfortune' as she called it, of having seven sons. Yet, she did not treat them as 'presidents' but rather inculcated in them a sense of responsibility both at home and outside it. She had to:

> ... [T]each them to pound maize, wash plates and clean the house. I would even send them to the maize mill and to draw water. If I had listened to suggestions that boys should not be given girls' jobs, I would not be walking now. My back would have been broken by now. But as you can see, I can walk.

Furthermore, changes to the modes of production as typified by the shift from subsistence agriculture to a cash economy have exploded the belief that only male children will acquire the capacity to help their families. Since access to cash is now determined by the extent of schooling that one undertakes, it is becoming more widely recognised that the better the opportunities that are given to *all* children within the family, the more extensive the network of resources to which the parents or guardians will have access in old age. Consequently, it serves the parents' and guardians' interests not to discriminate against any children that are under their care.

Yet another source of motivation is religious or spiritual conviction. Although most of the Lomwe profess some form of religious faith and are members of one of the various Christian denominations or Islamic sects operating in Thyolo District, they are also a deeply spiritual people. Consequently, the worship of the Biblical and Koranic God is undertaken alongside observation and ceremony honouring the spirits of the ancestors. Integral to these religious and spiritual activities is adherence to various moral codes that demand treating fellow human beings with kindness and fairness.

Another basis for non-discrimination perspectives is the knowledge of children's rights principles, and in particular, of provisions proscribing discrimination against

---

[7] *Yaya* is a term of endearment for a grandmother (perhaps corresponding to nan in the English language). I visited Yaya on several occasions but she never told me her name, insisting that Yaya was sufficient.

children. In this regard, it is noteworthy that the majority of the young participants knew and could recite a significant number of the principles that are contained in the African Children's Charter. This is because children's rights are taught (if not always followed) as part of the social studies course both in primary as well as secondary school. Parents, guardians and children who do not attend school have also gained knowledge relating to the rights and welfare of the child through the activities of the Mai Nahipa and Ulendo Arts Theatre who frequently hold discussion groups, performances and recitals at the court of Village Head Ndalama. The radio has also proved very informative in relaying children's rights messages. Thus, through these various means, a significant number of children as well as their parents and guardians have come to know of the non-discrimination principle as part of the law of the land that governs relationships between children and their guardians.

It is clear from the foregoing that the principle of non-discrimination has a place within Lomwe cultural space. However, it is also apparent that its legitimacy remains contested. It is in the interests of children's rights practitioners to maintain this contestability because this presents an opportunity for challenging attitudes that encourage discrimination against children. The many bases of perspectives that support non-discrimination present opportunities for tackling inconsistent practices.

Best Interests: Tracing the Contours of a Shadow-Less Concept

The African Children's Charter enshrines what is commonly known as the welfare or best interests principle. It provides that:

> In all actions concerning the child undertaken by any person or authority, the best interests of the child shall be the primary consideration (African Children's Charter 1990: art. 4).

The best interests principle appears in a variety of contexts throughout the Charter. In particular, it is used in relation to the child's freedom of thought, conscience and religion (African Children's Charter 1990: art. 9), with reference to the child's right to the enjoyment of parental care and protection (African Children's Charter 1990: art. 19), in relation to the parental responsibility for the upbringing of the child (African Children's Charter 1990: art. 20), in relation to the system of adoption or similar practices (African Children's Charter 1990: art. 24), and in relation to measures pursued in the case of children who are permanently or temporarily deprived of their family environment (African Children's Charter 1990: art. 25).

Article 4(1), as just quoted, provides that the best interests principle shall be treated as the primary consideration 'in *all* actions concerning the child undertaken by any person or authority'. This phrase provides significant guidance as to what constitutes the scope of the provision. The reference to 'all actions concerning children' emphasises the fact the principle is meant to be applied widely. In fact, it must be applied in every case where the rights and welfare of the child are under consideration.

The preceding analysis clearly demonstrates that the best interests principle plays a central role in the application of the provisions contained in the African Children's Charter. If the Charter is to have any impact at all in the lives of African children, it is crucial that the principle should enjoy the same centrality in their day to day lives. In the following section, I outline the status of the best interests principle in the lives of children in Magombo and Ndalama village.

Lost in translation? Conceptualising best interests

Consideration of the principle within the Lomwe social context brings to the fore the difficulties with determining the exact scope and meaning of the principle. Chief amongst these difficulties is the conceptualisation of the principle in terms that accord it the same level of importance as is the case at international law. Fashioning a translation that effectively communicates the essence of the principle is a challenging if not impossible task. In this regard, it is worth noting that the Chichewa version of the CRC omits the principle in its entirety (UNICEF n.d). Consequently, during the early stages of the fieldwork, I employed the phrase *kuyika ana patsogolo* whose literal meaning is 'putting children first'. However, my conversations with Mai Nahipa, the children's rights specialist from Magombo village, revealed that my translation did not adequately cover the scope of the best interests principle. Her principal concern was that my translation did not sufficiently reflect the idea that the principle applied 'to all actions concerning children'. She, therefore, suggested that I adopt the phrase *kuyika zofunikira za ana patsogolo pa nkhani zonse zomwe zikuwakhudza* [putting the needs of children first in all matters that concern them]. Yet, despite expressing the best interests principle more clearly, the phrase is difficult to work with and proved problematic to introduce during normal conversation. I therefore reverted to *kuyika ana patsogolo* because of the idea of paramountcy that that phrase engendered.

Mai Nahipa further pointed out that although during her training as a children's rights facilitator within the two villages, the best interests principle was highlighted as forming the backbone of children's rights discourse, the principle was absent from the *Chichewa*-based materials that she was given to use in her advocacy work. She is the person who first alerted me to the absence of the principle in the *Chichewa* version of the CRC.

My conversations with primary and secondary school students also revealed a lack of knowledge relating to this most famous of children's rights principles. Although students had been taught many aspects of children's rights and could recite the various rights with ease, the best interests principle remained unknown.

Yet, Mai Nahipa points out that, although there are problems in emphasising the principle in the same terms as is the case under the African Children's Charter, this factor alone does not water down the importance of the principle or suggest that little could be gained by pursuing efforts aimed at its popularisation. She points out that the best interests is more about *zochitika* ['doing' or 'the real stuff'] and less about *pakamwa* ['the mouth' or 'talking']. She says:

> It is difficult to teach others about what the best interests principle is. However, it is not as difficult to demonstrate how the principle should apply in the upbringing of children ...Consider the case of the children that we have at the orphanage. We could easily have left them with their extended families. But doing so would have meant that they would have suffered hardship. They would not have been able to go to school or have enough food and clothes. Although it is always nice to be with one's relatives, it is better for these children to live here with us.

Thus, according to Mai Nahipa, one should worry less about translations and focus more on the real lives of particular children and determine a course of action that best serves their needs. But the question remains: how does one discuss the concept in Lomwe cultural space?

However, it is not just the technical difficulties of translation that make the observation of the best interests principle very complicated. Rather, it is the proposed primacy of the principle and its focus on the individual child's interests that creates problems, for there are other interests that compete with and are considered more urgent than the child's interests. The general Lomwe worldview focuses on family or community interests rather than on the individual. In this regard, it is worth noting that individuals are generally not in a position to claim rights which are separate from and against the family or kinship group of which they are members. Consequently, children do not have special entitlements outside the welfare of the family as a whole. Yaya's views on the primacy of children's rights and interests captures this conception of entitlements very well:

> When one buys clothes or food for the children, he or she just buys. One does do not stop to consider each child individually. If there is no sugar at home, everyone will not have porridge that morning. If there is money in the home, then everyone will leave the home cheerfully in the morning. But if there is no money, we face it together.

'Facing it together' negates the whole idea of children's best interests being the primary consideration, since by definition primacy under the African Children's Charter requires that the child's interests take precedence. Yaya's views on the ordering of priorities in the home were echoed by other participants. For example, Mai Namame argues that placing the individual child's as *primary* is akin to *kusankha* (discrimination) between family members, and as was argued earlier, *kusankha* is inherently un-Lomwe. She goes on to question the individual focus of children's rights by making observations on its impact on family unity:

> These freedoms that children are said to have nowadays are good but sometimes they cause problems. The unity and peace that was in the family is now gone and parents have no freedom any more.... According to our culture everyone should be similarly treated. You cannot take one member of the family and give them special treatment. Yet the freedoms which you describe, especially this one of putting children first requires that we should create gaps between each other. This will just lead to quarrelling within the family.

Clearly, then, achieving the acceptance of the best interests principle will not be an easy task. The concept is perceived as challenging the very foundation of family relationships which are based on co-existence and the sharing of both the good and the bad.

The child's best interests in family decision-making

The structure of Lomwe families has a profound influence on the decision-making process relating to children. Lomwe families are arranged along matrilineal lines. Consequently, adult males from the maternal family are the most influential persons in the decision-making processes relating to the child. Important issues such as those relating to children's education, choice of marriage partners and career paths are not the preserve of the immediate parents or guardians, let alone the children themselves. Since relationships are constructed along the extended family model, various family units are aggregated together along kinship lines to form clans. This system of integration allows a large number of people to be incorporated into the family circle. The aggregation of persons is also matched by a similar diffusion of duties and rights. This arrangement of family relationships has several implications for the best interests of children.

One such implication is the idea that the child belongs to the family or the kinship group. Consequently, parental rights and authority are exercised by a large number of people each one of whom is entitled to make or contribute to decisions relating to the child's best interests. Under this family system, a child has a number of 'fathers' and 'mothers'. For example, all the brothers and male cousins of the biological father are considered the fathers of the child whilst the mother's sisters and female cousins are regarded as mothers. Although there may be no genetic ties between the child and a particular father or mother, the exercise of parental authority for these social fathers and mothers is real. In other words, in terms of the exercise of parental authority, there are no distinctions between the biological mother and father and those accorded such status through extended kinship relations.

Related to the idea that the child belongs to everyone is the principle that decisions affecting the child cannot be taken by one person even when they are the biological parent or the immediate guardian. There is an expectation by members of the extended family who are entitled to exercise parental rights and duties over that particular child to be consulted in making decisions and choices for that child.

In response to population mobility and changes in settlement patterns, the principle of dispersed parental authority has not been restricted to clan relations. Through the migration of individuals from their villages of origin to places far from their local kin, parents and guardians have found the concept useful in relation to neighbours and friends. Consequently, it is not unusual for parents to delegate and for neighbours to assume parental duties and rights. In some cases, neighbours assume such parental rights and duties even in the absence of direct delegation with full confidence that the parents will approve of the decisions they make.

However, this type of decision-making process does not always serve the best interests of the child. In the first place, since a large number of persons are entitled to make decisions, conflicting solutions to particular problems may arise and it is not always possible to get decisions made as quickly as possible because of the large number of opinions to be solicited even when the best interests of the child require a quick resolution. One obvious example of the latter are decisions relating to the custody of orphans. Family procedures usually make the process very drawn out as an aspect of respect to the dead parents, when a quick resolution would be best for the children.

The second implication of the extended family's structure on deciding the child's best interests relates to the manner in which decisions relating to children's issues are made. In this regard, it should be noted that a person's status as adult or a child has implications for the entitlements that he or she may claim. In particular, it was demonstrated that the acquisition of voice and authority is directly related to one's position in the family hierarchy. As a result, the nature of the relationship between children and those who exercise parental rights often serves to articulate the views of adults without equal regard to those of children. In particular, the relationship between children and their parents is marked with a certain distance and an air of deference. Indeed, during socialisation the ethos of unquestioned respect towards elders is emphasised. One practical consequence of the ethic of respect is that children do not represent themselves on the family council, membership of which is only achieved through the ascription of status related to the achievement of adulthood. The importance of respect is evident from the large number of pulpits from which the message of respect is preached.

The child's duty to respect parents at all times (African Children's Charter 1990: art. 31) is based on the assumption that parents and guardians always act in the best interests of children. Consequently, the child's contribution to the decision-making process is suppressed. In a nutshell, the quest for a course of action that serves children's interests is conducted in a manner that promotes adult views of what they feel those interests should be. Whilst this style of decision-making is capable of protecting children's interests, less insistence on respect and its association with silence could improve the process.

The third implication of the communal nature of the extended family system relates to the pre-eminence of family interests over all other interests. In the event of disharmony between the interests of the child and those of the family, custom holds that the latter will trump the former. The principal rationale for this is that the family is regarded as a protective place for all its members and as such, decisions that promote its welfare as a whole will also automatically protect that of its individual members. Consequently, the idea of an individual child's interests gaining paramountcy does not sit well with this logic of inclusiveness. In the majority of cases, choices that further family interests will also favour the best interests of the child. For example, nowadays it is recognised that in order for a child to effectively execute his or her duty of providing support for the family, he or she must attend school. Consequently, parents and guardians make the effort to ensure that children stay in school. In the result, both the family interests as well as the child's interests are preserved. However, where there is conflict, it is obvious that the child's needs have to be suspended.

In closing this subsection, it may be noted that efforts aimed at securing the child's best interests are bound up with the arrangements surrounding the home, kinship ties and decision-making procedures that inform these relationships. Whereas there is a clear recognition that children's interests are an important issue in the management of the family, the customary processes for mediating those interests tend to serve interests 'larger' than those of the individual children. In a way, therefore, the practical difficulties in pin-pointing where the best interests of children lie within Lomwe cultural space mirror the philosophical dilemmas that were highlighted at the beginning of this section.

The primacy of family interests is so well entrenched that the idea of the child's individual interests trumping those is pathologised as being akin to discrimination or *kusankha*. Consequently, the popularisation of the best interests principle as a leading child-rearing tool within Lomwe society must be expected to encounter significant resistance.

Survival and Development and the Interrelatedness of Children's Rights

Article 5(1) of the African Children's Charter provides that every child has an inherent right to life and that this right must be protected by law. Article 5(2) complements the recognition of this right by obliging states to ensure to the maximum extent possible the survival, protection and development of the child. Since the right to life and the right to survival are essential preconditions to the enjoyment of any of the rights protected in the African Children's Charter, they apply in all considerations relating to the promotion and protection of the rights and welfare of the child. In other words, the right to survival and development is a general principle that serves to reinforce the *raison d'être* of each of the rights enshrined in the Charter.

The survival and development principle enunciated in article 5 of the African Children's Charter engenders two separate but closely related concepts, namely, the right to survival and the right to development. The right to survival is a dynamic concept and incorporates all the necessary steps that a state party must undertake in order to ensure the healthy development of children. Clearly, then, the duty on states parties to ensure to the maximum extent possible the survival and development of the child highlights particular aspects of the right to life. In other words, the codification of the right to survival represents an acknowledgement that rights which protect aspects of a child's survival are interrelated and cannot be protected in isolation (van Bueren 1995: 293). The African Children's Charter reinforces this ideal by making particular provision which protects these interrelated aspects. The Charter achieves this by including within its ambit protections for basic survival needs such as the right to health, the right to adequate nutrition and safe drinking water (African Children's Charter 1990: art 14), and the right to be protected from customs and practices that are prejudicial to the child's life or health (African Children's Charter 1990: art 21).

The right to development, on the other hand, refers to the right of individuals, groups and peoples to participate in, contribute to, and enjoy continuous economic, social, political and cultural development in which all human rights can be realised. The right to development is, therefore, a dynamic concept that stresses the importance of fostering and nurturing the many dimensions of the child. The African Children's Charter concretises this approach by protecting rights and freedoms that enhance the child's developmental attributes. These include guarantees relating to the child's right to education (African Children's Charter 1990: art 11); the right to rest and leisure, to engage in play and recreational activities, and to participate freely in cultural life and the arts (African Children's Charter 1990: art 12); the right to be protected from all forms of economic exploitation and from performing any work that is likely to be hazardous or interfere with the child's physical, mental, spiritual, moral or social development (African Children's Charter 1990: art 25). In addition, the Charter makes special provision for the development of disabled children by obliging states to provide special care and assistance appropriate to the child's condition in a manner conducive to the child achieving the fullest possible social integration, individual development and his cultural and moral development (African Children's Charter 1990: art 13).

By recognising the fundamental interdependence of various aspects of the child's life, the survival and development principle highlights the unity of purpose of the African Children's Charter's substantive as well as procedural provisions. The principle does not create new rights for children but merely serves to emphasise the holistic approach that must be followed in the promotion and protection of the rights and welfare of the child. Each one of the elements of the child's survival and development is equally important and states parties should strive to protect them all. For example, it would be counterproductive to protect the girl child from early marriage practices[8] without providing her with sufficient and accessible means to acquire an education.

Children's survival and development: Partnerships and resource networks

Due to the broad scope of survival and development rights, the realisation of this principle entails satisfying a whole range of civil and political as well as economic, social and cultural rights. As a result, it takes a multifaceted approach employing different types of legal, economic, political as well as social resources and skills to guarantee these rights. As a matter of necessity, it requires the establishment of workable partnerships between various stakeholders in society, all of whom direct their efforts towards the achievement of the promotion and protection of the rights and welfare of the child. The state is one of these partners. But perhaps the most important partner of all is the family.

In the context of a developing country economy such as Malawi's, the state is often not in a position to guarantee children essential social welfare services such as free education, free health services, adequate nutrition or access to a reasonable

[8] Early marriage is described as "another serious problem which some girls, as opposed to boys, must face". See Office of the High Commissioner for Human Rights n.d.: 17.

standard of housing. Consequently, most of the responsibility for providing these essential aspects of the child's survival and development falls on individual families. In other words, there exists a partnership between the state and individual family units for ensuring that children's survival and development rights are realised. In this regard, the state through its civil and criminal laws and through the limited provision of social welfare services endeavours to fulfil its obligations. For its part, the family complements these efforts by providing the emotional and material needs of the child. How effectively the family fulfils this role is a function of its perception of the obligations towards children as well as the level of economic resources that it has at its disposal.

The first factor does not pose significant problems, largely because of the conception of childhood. As was discussed earlier, the child is considered a gift and someone who is entitled to special treatment. Consequently, under Lomwe tradition, the family regards itself as being responsible for the survival and development of the child by ensuring that the child is fed, dressed, educated and in good health. However, the level of economic resources at the disposal of the family is closely tied to the structure of kin relationships which in turn affects the type of resource networks that children have for their survival and development rights. In this context, a 'resource network' denotes a concentration of financial, economic, social, emotional, political and informational resources to which members of that network can turn for the satisfaction of different needs.

In this regard, the extended family offers access to different types of resources and capacities for the children within it. Since the guiding principle is that the child belongs to the whole family, it is not uncommon for a child to be looked after by his or her 'other fathers and mothers' on account of the inability so to do by his immediate parents. Parents realise the importance of this duty and children recognise and often enforce their entitlement to be supported by members of the extended family. For example, Caesar Muluta, a member of the focus group from Thyolo Secondary School, does not get financial support for his education at the secondary school from his parents. Rather, it is his elder sister's husband who provides everything for him and to all intents and purposes acts as his parent. Caesar does not need to ask for support, for his sister's husband is well aware of his responsibilities.

The duty to support all children within the extended family is not restricted to the provision of economic support but also extends to the provision of moral, spiritual and emotional support. This wide ranging focus on areas of support ensures the well-rounded growth of children who will eventually become well-adjusted adults. For example, when John Biswick's fourteen year-old son became unruly and violent at home, his wife suggested that they send him to the wife's sister's home for a few months. Recalling the incident, he says:

> I had tried all options to discipline him but had failed.... It got to the point where he would deliberately engage in discourteous behaviour and then challenge me to chastise him.... I sent him to his younger mother for about four months. When he came back, he was a changed person. All the bad traits that he had demonstrated after getting initiated were gone.

Thus, the extended family system serves to provide a robust network of resources that is able to handle the different needs of children as they grow up. However, this capacity has become tested in contemporary times through changes in the means of economic production and the resultant adjustments in the social organisation of the extended family. The extended family's resource network is premised on the proximity of family members. As individual family units have dispersed in search of jobs, marriage and other things, the ability of the extended family to guarantee children's survival and development rights has suffered some strain.

Consequently the nuclear family has shot into prominence. More and more, children's survival and development rights have become the responsibility of the immediate family. The resource network to which children have access has been reduced, with dramatic effect on the prospects of children's survival and development. Mai Nahipa's observation that 'there never used to be orphans in Ndalama and Magombo village' exemplifies the situation. It is not the case that there were no orphans, but that the resource network used to be robust enough to take care of them. The rising number of orphans is merely a symptom of the breakdown of these networks, as is the incidence of child labour.

Having regard to the unequivocal obligations that the state has assumed in respect of children's survival and development rights, one would have assumed that the state would step into the breach and supplement where the family is failing. However, the state's intervention has been less than effective and many children still continue to live on the margins. In order to mitigate the consequences of shrinking resource networks and the absence of credible partners, families have developed some supplementary networks which carry the burden traditionally borne by the extended family system. The supplementary networks include: friendships;

communal relationships such as those between church members, workmates or neighbours; and informational networks such as gossip networks at the local beer garden or common water source. All of these networks carry the burden for ensuring the survival and development of the child and are premised on the family's obligation to care for its young.

Although there is clear acceptability of the survival and development rights of the child, the manner in which the relevant provisions of the African Children's Charter will be realised in relation to each individual child depends on the strength of the resource network to which such child has access. If it is weak, then it is more likely than not that she may not enjoy protection from discrimination, or that her participation or survival and development rights will not be protected. Access to a network of resources gives the child power. It provides the ability to insist that her best interests are protected. Without the empowering presence of a resource network, the rights and welfare of the child are liable to be violated. In this regard, it is clear that the state should do more in honouring its side of the partnership with the family. Failure to do so is forcing many children to live on the margins of society.

Participation: A Brief Introduction

There are several participation provisions in the African Children's Charter, which provides:

> Every child who is capable of communicating his or her own views shall be assured the right to express his opinions freely in all matters and to disseminate his opinions subject to such restrictions as are prescribed by laws (African Children's Charter 1990: art. 7).

This provision is supplemented by article 4(2) which guarantees that:

> In all judicial or administrative proceedings affecting a child who is capable of communicating his or her own views, an opportunity shall be provided for the views of the child to be heard either directly or through an impartial representative as a party to the proceedings, and those views shall be taken into consideration by

> the relevant authority in accordance with the provisions of appropriate law (African Children's Charter 1990: art. 4(2)).[9]

The participation principle applies to *all* matters including judicial and administrative proceedings. It therefore cuts across the whole spectrum of issues relating to the rights and welfare of the child, qualifying as a general principle which should be considered in all matters relating to the protections provided by the African Children's Charter. Clearly, therefore, the participation principle is a lynchpin in the scheme set up by the Charter. Yet accounts of children's rights in Africa often highlight the absence or restriction of these rights for children (e.g. Chirwa 2002: 157; Himonga 1998: 95). In this regard, a considerable proportion of the accounts emphasise the place of respect in relations between children and adults. This picture, however, is only partially correct and represents only part of the mosaic that is children's participation.

The right to participation is perhaps the best known children's rights principle. In local terms, it is known as *ufulu wamwana wolankhula za kukhosi* (or the right of the child to speak his or her mind). In the local language, the phrase *kulankhula za kukhosi* or speaking one's mind is very descriptive, carrying the image of someone giving vent to something that could otherwise choke them. The right to freedom of expression is therefore loved by many children because of the notion of freedom that it engenders and loathed by conservative adults because of the seeds of rebellion that it apparently sows.

The oft-cited aphorism that children should be seen and not heard is not representative of the practice in Lomwe society. Since socialisation principally

[9] The other participation provisions include article 8 which guarantees the child freedom of association; article 9 on the child's right to freedom of thought, conscience and religion and article 12 which enshrines the child's right to participate freely in cultural life and the arts. Article 13(1) and 27(2) provide specific detail on the participatory rights of disabled children and children in conflict with the law, respectively. Curiously, however, the African Children's Charter does not make provision for the right to seek, receive and impart information even though this is an integral part of the participation rights regime under the African Charter of Human and People's Rights, art 9(1). The participation principle is also a key theme in the Protocol to the African Charter on Human and Peoples' Rights on the Rights of Women in Africa (2000: preamble, arts 9, 10, 17, 18, 19, 23).

relies on oral traditions, it is almost axiomatic that talking between adults and children cannot be avoided. Consequently, there exist various channels of communication between children and adults. Whilst the existence of these modes of communication is not always indicative that children's views were taken into account, it nevertheless provides evidence that children were not only seen but also heard. Participants cited various arrangements intended to enable children express their views. These included play (which incorporates various modes of expression such as song and dance, recitals and role play), direct communication to parents, and communication through intermediaries. I examine these different types of communication and their role in aiding children's participation below.

Children's play is more than mere amusement and can sometimes convey messages to parents. According to Yaya:

> A good parent knows that it is important to lend a good ear to what children are doing outside because through their various activities, one is able to gauge whether they are happy or sad. This is especially necessary in the case of the girls. If during *fulaye*[10] one gentleman's name keeps popping up, or if during tug-of-war, your daughter's friends keep pairing her up with a certain boy, a good parent knows that it is about time you checked her room and prevent events from overtaking you.

This mode of communication was also used to relay important messages. For example, Patrick's mother recalls that Patrick used role play to complain about his father's drink-induced abusiveness:

> He would sometimes be the father. He would pretend to be drunk and scold his 'child' in a very harsh manner. I talked to my *ankhoswe*[11] to tell his father about it.... Things did change, at least for a while.

In addition to role-playing, song and dance is also used to communicate with elders. Parents often convey instructions to young people in performances during

---

[10] *Fulaye* is a two team game mainly played by girls and which involves one player dodging a ball thrown players of the other team.

[11] Marriage counselor or advisor.

special ceremonies such as those celebrating the birth of a child, a marriage or during initiation. Children are also able to use this mode of communication either during play or initiation ceremonies.

Although the means of communication related to play are often unstructured and may yield no response from the adults concerned, they still represent an important repertoire in the exchange of opinions between parents and children. In a society where respect and distance are expected, this means of communication offers an option to children and their guardians.

Another method of getting children's input into the family decision-making process is through the deployment of intermediaries. In particular, communication through grandparents was identified by many participants as constituting the most reliable channel for children's participation. It is noteworthy that the relationship between children and grandparents is characterised by feelings of friendship and openness. Oftentimes, a child will be closer to the grandparent than he or she is to the parents. Consequently, many important issues, including those considered too taboo to be the subject of a polite conversation between a child and his parents, are proper subjects of conversation between children and their grandparents. The robust nature of this relationship serves to convey important messages during socialisation such as those relating to honour, loyalty, sacrifice, and duty. This is done through the recital of fables, recollections of family traditions and proverbs or simply by letting the child sit through conversations involving the grandparent and his or her friends.

The close relationship between village head Magombo and his daughter's nine year old son, Fred, is typical of these relationships. Describing Fred as his brother, he says:

> When I hold court, I make sure he is at my side as long as he is not in school. His mother is somewhat strict with him and he may be too scared to ask questions of her.... During court hearings, he sits quietly and listens but once the visitors are gone, the questions begin. When he goes for initiation, he will not be totally uninformed like his peers.

Another example is that of Esnath Minjere, who elected to discuss the details of her pregnancy with her grandfather only and refused to talk about it with the female members of her family.

Another important intermediary is the mother. A child's relationship with the mother is not only very respectful but also very intimate. Mai Sambalikagwa observes of her relationship with her daughter who is now married:

> She is like my sister. We tell each other *zapantondo*[12]. Before she got married and was still our responsibility, I made sure that her father knew of her needs.... She was a very shy girl and would not sit in the same room as her father.

In some respects, the mother's relationship with her children, especially girls, mirrors that between a grandparent and his or her grandchildren. The major difference is that, because of the patriarchal set-up of the family, women who are not advanced in age do not have as much influence on the family decision-making process as do the men or family patriarchs. Consequently, the mother's role in facilitating participation is sometimes limited.

It is therefore clear from the foregoing that the existence of various forms of communication channels demonstrates that Lomwe custom does not prohibit children from expressing themselves. In addition, the wide ranging scope of the kind of matters that could be addressed through these mechanisms indicates that children's participation is not restricted to mundane matters but also includes important issues such as those pertaining to marriage, custody and others. The existence of a rigid repertoire relating to children's participation supports the view that under custom children do not have the freedom to express their views at any time or any place, but by the same token does not indicate the absence of participation structures. The importance of this observation is that the participation rights of the child detailed in the African Children's Charter are not out of place within Lomwe society.

The channels of communication detailed above worked well in traditional society when the extended family lived in close proximity and family decision-making was more or less centralised. However, changes in socio-economic patterns and the resultant mobility of rural folk have impacted on these various modes of participation. One of the most obvious changes is the need for direct communication between children and decision makers within the family. In the following section, I discuss how these changes have affected the participation rights

[12] Tales from the maize mill-denotes gossip and other juicy stories.

of the child and how family discourse has responded to such changes.

Adaptation and resistance: A tale of rudeness and freedom

For the past one hundred and fifty years or so, the traditional Lomwe social structure has had to contend with and in some cases yield to the changes brought about by Christianity, colonialism, independence, democracy, human rights and globalisation. The impact of these various changes on the manner in which the family handles its affairs has been profound. Where a community is organised on the basis of sharing and mutual support, the interests of individual members are subsumed or aggregated with those of the group. Under these circumstances, individual interests are not loudly articulated and this tends to minimise the risk of conflict between group interests and those of the individual (Rwezaura 1998: 84). With such a relatively harmonious social co-existence, the individual's direct participation in important decision making is not seen as crucial in protecting his or her interests. The interests of the community and those of the individual are so interwoven that community leaders who assume the role of decision-makers can be trusted to determine at a general level what best serves the interests of all including children without needing to solicit their views.

However, the social forces that were detailed above have upset this equilibrium. One evident effect of these socio-economic changes in Magombo and Ndalama village is the mobility of family members in search of jobs, marriages and the attractions of a twenty-first century economy. It is therefore the case that children no longer live in the same households as their grandparents. Regular contact between children and their grandparents, which is the bedrock of the latter's intermediary function, is no longer guaranteed. In these two villages, a significant proportion of the village folk are not originally from the village. Many came to Thyolo district to look for work at the nearby tea factories as well as at the government departments at the *Boma*.

Furthermore, the changes in living arrangements have also affected the transmission of the art of communication through song and dance. Irregular contacts between children and the 'bearers' of tradition has meant that the opportunity to learn about these modes of communication is sometimes lost. Contemporary consumption patterns have also affected the relationship between children's participation through song and dance. With western music forms taking hold over many youngsters, the art of imaginative discourse through music, poetry and dance is slowly slipping away.

Thus, changes in the social organisation of the family have profoundly affected the structures that facilitated children's participation. These changes have made it necessary for supplementary or alternative structures of communication to be developed and utilised. One of these supplementary structures is exemplified by the demands for direct participation. These demands have been bolstered by at least two factors: necessity and the awareness of children's rights.

In the first place, the metamorphosis of the extended family from a close-knit centralised unit to far flung family units has made the representation models for effecting children's participation somewhat inefficient in executing that role. Consequently, it has become necessary for persons that are directly responsible for the child's daily care to provide the participation structures. This state of affairs has elevated the importance of the nuclear family which has found itself at the centre of the child's participation needs. However, since most parents were brought up under the traditional representation participation regime, they are ill-equipped to handle these new family dynamics.

Secondly, the awareness of the child's participation rights has encouraged children to demand that they be allowed 'to speak out what is in their throats'. Recognising the importance of respect between the generations, children are increasingly insisting that their respect will be earned once they are given the opportunity to express their views. However, demands such as these fly in the face of the unequivocal principle of respect for elders at all times (African Children's Charter 1992: art 31(a)).

Consequently, parents increasingly see the assertiveness now prevalent in their children as evidence of the moral breakdown of society attributable to the neglect of the old way of doing things. In response to the perceived 'rudeness' of their children, some parents insist that the traditional modes of participation should be emphasised and that the idea that children should be allowed to air their views is too disruptive to be allowed to take root. John Monjeza is one such parent and he puts across his views in the following manner:

> Nowadays, if you ask your own child to carry out a little errand for you, he will refuse and tell you in the face that it is his freedom to refuse and yet another freedom to inform you of his refusal. During our time, one could not even think of such a

> response for fear your thoughts could be heard. If I had dared answer my father in such a manner, I would have been sent for initiation for a second time in order to be taught good manners. Democracy[13] has brought good things but it has also brought so much disrespect.... One could beat this rudeness out of the young people but who wants a visit from the police? It seems to me that democracy is good but only for the young ones.

The equating of the child's participation rights with rudeness has built resistance to the idea that children are entitled to freedom of expression. Thus, parents whose reference point is the traditional model of participation, see the demands for direct participation as a species of discourtesy.

In reaction, this stance has made children's demands for parents and people in authority to respect the right to air one's views even more insistent. For the children, whose point of reference is democracy, freedom and human rights, the reference to the traditional modes of expression seems overly restrictive and inconsistent with the idea of being free. Unedited excerpts from an essay entitled 'Should parents listen to their children' written by Laudon Samson from Thyolo Secondary School captures the frustrations of both parents and children in the attempts by both camps to navigate the treacherous minefield of participation rights in the context of entrenched views on respect and 'proper' modes of child participation:

> The parents should not listen to their children just because she/he is young or the children are younger than the parents, so they think that the children cannot talk any wise or meaningful to them since they are young....
>
> The parents should not listen to their children due to the history of children nowadays... the majority of them are smoking... Indian hemp, drinking beer and [taking] drugs. So these things makes the parents to think that children cannot talk anything helpful [and] as a result, they don't listen to them.

[13] The era of human rights and democracy talk dawned at the same time in Malawi. Consequently the two ideas are sometimes used interchangeably.

> Other parents listen to their children but they don't use the things that the children talk to them, because they think that if they use the advice or the things that they heard from their children, those children would think that they are superior. As a result the parents just listen but they don't use it.
>
> Some parents are so cruel and when their children talk to them they start shouting because they think that they are being rude and that since they are grown ups, they should not listen to their children. Some parents even [go to the extent] of chasing their children away from their home.
>
> Other parents listen to their children but at the end they ask you questions. For example, they ask you questions like these: What makes you say so? Who told you to do that? What was your expectation about that? So these questions interfere with the children's [efforts] to talk to them and as a result the children think that the parents do not listen to them.
>
> Some parents accept the advice... their children talk to them but are minor in number and they thank their children about the things they talk to them about.

The essay demonstrates the differing entry points into the issue of participation by both children and parents. At first glance, it may seem that traditional perspectives on participation and the new ideas related to 'democracy' and children's rights are far apart. At the rhetorical level, there is no obvious consensus, with parents decrying the unbelievable insolence of children and the children failing to understand their parents' old-fashioned ways. However, the fact that many families have not been thrown into a crisis is indicative of the fact that the two paradigms are interacting in a manner that is not fatal to family harmony.

The crucial point evident from this is that as long as there is a basis for children's participation within Lomwe society, arguments about the exact nature of those participation structures are essentially non-fatal, and sooner or later there will be a resolution. The challenge is ensuring that such a resolution favours the promotion and protection of children's rights.

Concluding Remarks: Children's Rights in Cultural Practice

The protection and promotion of the rights and welfare of the African child is in large part about influencing the day to day child rearing practices of families. If the intention of ensuring the best protection for each and every African boy or girl is to be achieved, the principles of the African Children's Charter must be translated into practice on the ground. The preceding analysis of the Charter's general principles brings into sharp relief the importance of existing cultural logics and categories in the acceptance or rejection of the various principles that make up the international children's rights corpus. The existence of child-rearing practices that are akin to or supportive of particular principles make arguments in favour of introducing or adopting the 'new' principles easier since the relevance of those principles is already culturally accepted. In other words, the cultural legitimacy of children's rights norms is easier to establish in situations where local practice has already laid the ground work for appropriation.

However, even where there are existing narratives which are supportive of children's rights practice, the process is not straight-forward nor predictable. The local appropriation of a transnational institution such as children's rights transforms underlying cultural categories and practices. However, at the same time, the appropriated institution is itself adapted and sometimes radically transformed. As parents and children such as those in Magombo and Ndalama village seek ways of combining their conceptions of family practice and children's rights norms, they not only redefine their cultural landscape but they also redefine the international children's rights corpus itself. Consequently, the image of children's rights that emanates from the process is a rich mosaic of local practice infused with international imperatives. It, therefore, goes without saying that any analysis of this process should avoid essentialising culture or children's rights as constituting strict categories (Merry 2001: 50). Rather than portraying culture and children's rights as exemplifying a conflict between universalist and relativist world views, the data from the fieldwork ably demonstrates that "culture is a field of creative interchange and contestation, often around shared symbols, propositions or practices" (Cowan et al. 2001: 5).

In seeking to determine the cultural legitimacy of the rights and welfare of the child, investigation into such shared symbols, propositions and practices requires a methodology which focuses on detailed case studies so that an analysis of child rearing practice and its intersection with culture and children's rights is not formulated in abstract forms but is located in specific, concrete experiences derived from the lives of children and their families. This requires a deconstruction of the conception of 'child' as a universal and homogeneous category and a consideration of children as rooted in specific cultural and historic categories. The African Children's Charter's insistence on culture and context is supportive of this type of methodology. It is a methodology which is sensitive to context, raises the legitimacy of the principles underlying the children's rights system, and gives rise to a pluralism that is neither universalist nor relativist but grounded in the reality of children's daily lives.

References

AFRICAN CHILDREN'S CHARTER
1990 *African Charter on the Rights and Welfare of the Child.* OAU Doc. CAB/LEG/24.9/49, adopted July 1990, entered into force 29 November 1999.

AFRICAN CHILDREN'S COMMITTEE (AFRICAN COMMITTEE OF EXPERTS ON THE RIGHTS AND WELFARE OF THE CHILD)
n.d. *Guidelines for Initial Reports of States Parties,* Cmtee/ACRWC/2 II.Rev2. Available at: http://www.africa-union.org/child/Guidelines%20for%20Initial%20reports%20 %20English.pdf (accessed 22 December 2008).

BAYEFSKY, Anne F.
1990 'The principle of equality or non-discrimination in international law' *Human Rights Journal* 11: 1-34.

BHALOTRA, Sonia
2003 'Child labour in Africa' OECD Social Employment and Migration Working Paper No. 4 OECD Publishing.

CHIRWA, Danwood Mzikenge
2002 'The merits and demerits of the African Charter on the Rights and Welfare of the Child' *International Journal of Children's Rights* 10: 157.

COMAROFF, John L. and Simon ROBERTS
1981 *Rules and Processes: The Cultural Logic of Dispute in an African Context,* Chicago: University of Chicago Press.

COWAN, Jane K., Marie-Bénédicte DEMBOUR and Richard A. WILSON
2001 'Introduction.' Pp. 1-25 in Jane K. Cowan, Marie Bénédicte Dembour and Richard A. Wilson (eds.), *Culture and Rights: Anthropological Perspectives.* Cambridge: Cambridge University Press.

GRIFFITHS Anne
2001 'Gendering culture: Towards a plural perspective on Kwena women's rights.' Pp. 102-126 in Jane K. Cowan, Marie Bénédicte Dembour and Richard A. Wilson (eds.), *Culture and Rights: Anthropological Perspectives*. Cambridge: Cambridge University Press.
GRIFFITHS, John
1986 'What is legal pluralism?' *Journal of Legal Pluralism* 24: 1-55.
HANNERZ, Ulf
1992 *Cultural Complexity: Studies in the Social Organizations of Meaning*, New York: Colombia University Press.
HIMONGA, Chuma
1998 'The right of the child to participate in decision-making: A perspective from Zambia.' Pp. 95-128 in Welshman Ncube (ed.) *Law, Culture, Tradition and Children's Rights in Eastern and Southern Africa.* Aldershot: Ashgate.
HELLUM, Anne
1999 *Women's Human Rights and Legal Pluralism in Africa: Mixed Norms and Infertility Management in Zimbabwe*. Oslo: Mond Books.
MACDONALD, Roderick A.
1998 'Metaphors of multiplicity: Civil society, regimes and legal pluralism.' *Arizona Journal of International and Comparative Law* 15: 69-91.
MERRY, Sally E.
2001 'Changing rights, changing culture.' Pp. 31-54 in Jane K. Cowan, Marie Bénédicte Dembour and Richard A. Wilson (eds.), *Culture and Rights: Anthropological Perspectives*. Cambridge: Cambridge University Press.
MNOOKIN, Robert H.
1975 'Child custody adjudication: Judicial functions in the face of indeterminacy.' *Law and Contemporary Problems* 39: 226-293.
PROTOCOL TO THE AFRICAN CHARTER ON HUMAN AND PEOPLES' RIGHTS ON THE RIGHTS OF WOMEN IN AFRICA
2000 *Protocol,* adopted 13 September 2000, entered into force 25 November 2005. CAB/LEG/66.6.
PRUETT, Marsha K., Kathy HOGAN-BRUEN and Tamara JACKSON.
2000 'The best interest of the child: Parents' versus attorneys' perspectives.' *Journal of Divorce and Remarriage* 33: 47-63.
ROBERTS, Simon
1979 *Order and Dispute*. New York: St Martin's Press.
RWEZAURA, Bart
1998 'The duty to hear the child: A view from Tanzania.' Pp. 57-94 in

Welshman Ncube (ed.) *Law, Culture, Tradition and Children's Rights in Eastern and Southern Africa.* Aldershot: Ashgate.

TAMANAHA, Brian Z.

1995 'An analytical map of social scientific approaches to the concept of law.' *Oxford Journal of Legal Studies* 15: 501-535.

UN COMMITTEE ON THE RIGHTS OF THE CHILD

2003 *General Comment No. 5: General measures of implementation for the Convention on the Rights of the Child (arts. 4, 42 and 44(6))* CRC/GC/2003/5. Available at: http://www.unhchr.ch/tbs/doc.nsf/(symbol)/CRC.GC.2003.5.En. (accessed 21 January 2009)

UNICEF

n.d. *Mgwirizano wa malamulo pa ufulu wachibadwidwe wa mwana*, Limbe: Montfort Press.

VAN BUEREN, Geraldine

1995 *International Law on the Rights of the Child.* Amsterdam: Kluwer Law Publishing.

WOODMAN, Gordon R.

1996 'Legal pluralism and the search for justice.' *Journal of African Law* 40: 152-167.

'NEITHER FISH NOR FOWL': AREA COURTS IN THE ILORIN EMIRATE IN NORTHERN NIGERIA

Abdulmumini A. Oba

Introduction

Law in Nigeria is a plural complex with the English style common law, Islamic law and the indigenous African law that goes under the name 'native law and custom' operating to various extents. This paper investigates the consequences for the Area Courts found in the Ilorin Emirate of northern Nigeria. Area Courts in northern Nigeria are the counterparts of southern Nigeria customary courts. They are the most heavily criticised of courts in Nigeria. They are frequently accused of incompetence, corruption, and arbitrariness (Odinkalu 1992). However, it is argued here that the basic problem with them, arising from the plural complex of laws in the country, is that they suffer from a crisis of identity; they are *de jure* secular courts but they are also historically and *de facto* 'religious' being Islamic courts. Though basically Islamic law courts, they partake of the other two laws.

The paper investigates the crisis of identity facing the courts and the ways and manners this has contributed to their problems. While doing this, it also assesses the extent to which the charges of inadequacy levelled generally against Area Courts hold true regarding Area Courts in the Ilorin Emirate. It concludes with suggestions of ways of improving the administration of justice in the Area Courts in the emirate and in Northern Nigeria in general.

The legal pluralism which is a prominent feature of the Nigerian legal system is fully represented in the Ilorin Emirate. The British colonial masters brought common law into Nigeria and into Ilorin following their conquest of the town in

1898. In the common law system, emphasis is on both the procedural and substantive aspects of law. Thus, common law is a very technical law in which lawyers play an important role, the emphasis being on technical or formal justice (Aguda 1986). It is generally expensive and time consuming.

Islamic law is an integral part of Islamic religion (Doi 1990: 2). Islamic law has been administered in northern Nigeria as far back as the 14th century. Of the four orthodox Islamic "schools of law" (Hanafi, Hanbali, Maliki and Shafi), Maliki Law is dominant in northern Nigeria. In Ilorin the consolidation of the Fulani hegemony by Shehu Alimi around 1807, and the incorporation of the town into the Sokoto Caliphate in 1828 assured the dominance of Islamic law in the town (Jimoh 1994: 35-67). However, Islamic law has not completely displaced customary law. There are pockets of traditional communities in the towns surrounding Ilorin. Many inhabitants of these towns still follow Yoruba traditions in their affairs.[1] Even in Ilorin town, customary law exists side by side with Islamic law (Elias 1971). In addition, the urbanisation of many of the towns in the emirate has meant an influx of other Nigerians from different cultural backgrounds.

The judicial process in traditional African communities was simple and speedy. Traditional African communities can be divided into two – the centralised states and the stateless. In the centralised communities, the traditional rulers played an important part in the administration of justice. In the stateless societies, the elders administered the law. In both types of communities, the supernatural – oaths, ordeals, ancestral spirits, and gods - played an important role (Oba 2002b). In civil disputes, reconciliation of the parties was the preferred objective. In more serious cases, punishment of the offender, spiritual cleansing of the community and compensation for the victim or the aggrieved party were the aims of the judicial process (Ayittey 1991: 39 – 69).

History and Structure of Area Courts

Prior to the advent of colonialism, as pointed out above, the Ilorin Emirate formed part of the Sokoto Caliphate established by Usman Dan Fodio. Islamic law was the applicable law of the Caliphate (Anderson 1978: 3). The Sokoto Caliphate itself inherited a strong Islamic learning tradition in the region of the Sudan (Tsiga and

[1] These towns include Afon, Laduba, Lasoju, Ilota, Egbejila, Lanwa, Jebba, Bode Saadu, Oke Oyi, Lajiki, Apado, and Malete (Kwara State Government n.d.).

Adamu 1997).

In the Sokoto Caliphate, each emir had his own court. Below the Emir, there were also alkali courts manned by learned jurists who were fluent in Arabic and who referred to Islamic law texts. Many scholars in the area wrote books on Islam generally and on Islamic law in particular (Shagari and Boyd 1978: 28–30. Murray Last 1977: 236–254, has a fairly comprehensive bibliography of these works.) These courts were highly sophisticated (Okonkwo and Naish 1980: 4), and applied Islamic law with the utmost vigour (Anderson 1978: 3). Islamic law is not applicable to non-Muslims (Said 1970: 152-154), to whom the courts apply the applicable customary (Anderson 1978: 172).

The colonial masters applying the system of indirect rule preserved the Alkali courts but gradually assumed control of their administration (Okany 1984: 10–17; Kumo 1988: 42-46). The courts administered both Islamic law and customary law under the direction of the colonial masters (Keay and Richardson 1966; Ubah 1982, 1985: 122-155). The Native Proclamation of 1900 was enacted for "the better regulation and control of native courts". It took control of the Alkali courts away from the Emirs and placed it in the hands of the Resident (Mahmud 1988: 9-11; Kumo 1988: 7 and 9). In 1933, the Native Courts Ordinance among other things changed their name to Native Courts. This position continued after independence until the Area Courts Edict, 1967 (now called the Area Courts Law, 1967) overhauled the Native Courts system. This Law among other things abolished the Emir's court and changed the name of Native Courts to Area Courts.

There are two types of Area Courts, Area Courts and Upper Area Courts (Area Courts Law, s. 17). An Area Court may consist of an area judge sitting alone or sitting with members provided that all questions of Islamic personal law are heard and determined by the area judge or any member learned in Islamic law sitting alone (Area Courts Law, s. 4). The appellate courts have insisted on a strict compliance with this provision by the Area Courts (*Kubra v Adeoti*; *Shittu v Shittu*; *Madiu v Baba*). The Area Courts are generally manned by single judges. The Upper Area Courts consisted of a President and two members, but now two members can constitute the court (Area Courts Law, s. 4(1), as amended by the Kwara State Law Revision (Miscellaneous Amendments) Law, 2006).

Area courts combine the administration of the three types of law (the common, Islamic, and customary laws) at the grassroots level. They are the courts of first instance with jurisdiction in civil cases relating to customary law and Islamic law.

They also have criminal jurisdiction. They administer the Penal Code and are guided for this purpose by the Criminal Procedure Code. The Penal Code is ultimately traceable to the English law of crimes (Karibi-Whyte 1993: 232; Owoade 1980: 25). All Islamic and customary law crimes have been abrogated by the Constitution (Constitution 1999, s. 36(12); *Aoko v Fagbemi)*. In some States in northern Nigeria, the administration of customary law is separated from that of Islamic law with Area Courts dealing with Islamic Law, and Customary Courts dealing with customary law (e.g. Customary Court of Appeal, 1979 (Plateau State), s. 2; *Usman v Umaru*). The fusion of administration of customary law and Islamic law in one set of courts was based on the colonial definition of 'native law and custom' as "including Moslem Law" (High Court Law, s. 2).

Parallel to the Area Courts are the Magistrate and District Courts. The Magistrate Courts deal with criminal cases, while the District Courts entertain only civil cases where the common law applies (Obilade 1979: 202-206). Appeals from Area Courts go to the Sharia Court of Appeal in matters of Islamic personal Law, that is, matters of marriage, inheritance, custody of children and *wakf* (Constitution, 1999, s. 277; Area Courts Law). In all other Islamic law matters, appeals go from the Area Court to the High Court (Area Courts Law, s. 54(2)). From both the Sharia Court of Appeal and the High Court, there are further appeals to the Court of Appeal from where appeal finally goes to the Supreme Court (Obilade 1979: 170-192; Constitution, 1999, ss. 233, 240, 244).

Crisis of Identity of Area Courts

One major reason for the crisis of identity facing Area Courts has to do with the religious nature of these courts. Odinkalu says that "one of the most popular misconceptions about the Area Courts is that they are religious courts" (Odinkalu 1992: 29). He argues that they are creations of statute and not religion. Odinkalu illustrates the 'misconception' with the following exchange between an Area Court judge and a legal practitioner:

> Judge: Lawyer, in the name of Allah, are you saying your client (the defendant) is not liable to pay the debt?
>
> Counsel: He is not liable being an agent, Mamman Daura ought to be liable.
>
> Judge: In the name of Allah, are you saying, under Islamic Law your client is not bound to pay the debt?

Counsel: Your worship, that seems to be the difference between this Court and I. The Court is thinking of Islamic Law while I have been arguing from the point of view of the ... [English] law of agency.

Judge: *La ila ila lah, Muhammadu Rausuulahi Salalahu alaihi wa salaam.*[2] You see, a Muslim lawyer saying that we cannot apply Islamic Law in Muslim land.

Court: *Allahu Akbar.*

This exchange between the court and counsel illustrates three fundamental crises of identity facing the court. The first is that the nature of Area Courts is not clear. Are they customary, Islamic or common law courts? Are they a hybrid of these three types of courts? The second is a crisis of identity facing Area Court judges. Are they Qadis in the traditional Islamic law sense or are they public servants? The third is a conflict of law problem, that is, which of the three types of laws apply in particular cases? Another crisis of identity that faced Area Court judges was whether they are civil servants or political appointees. These questions, their answers and consequences are explored hereunder.

Islamic, customary, or English law courts?

In the past the courts were manned by laymen who had basic training in Islamic law or were "versed in the customs of the people". Legal practitioners did not appear in the courts (Area Courts Law, s. 28(1)). Justice Karibi-Whyte, in justifying the non-applicability of the common law-based Evidence Act to Area Courts, articulated the rationale for barring legal practitioners from customary courts thus:

> Area Court judges are not learned in English Common law to enable them appreciate and understand provisions of the Evidence Law. Also in accordance with the section 28(a) of the Area Courts Edict, Legal Practitioners are barred from appearing to act for or assist any party before an Area Court. It is therefore important to insulate them from problems of misunderstanding, misapplication of the law and injustice that will inevitably arise if

[2] Translation: "There is no deity but Allah (God). Mohammed is His Messenger (May peace and blessing of Allah be upon him)" (Odinkalu 1992: 31).

> they, with all the above limitations, are bound to apply the Evidence Act. (*Kunso v Udo*: 55)

What his Lordship said here is *obiter* (by the way), it was not part of the *ratio* (binding parts) of the judgment. The position in Area Courts today differs from the above dictum in three major ways. First, the qualifications for appointments as Area Court judges have changed, legal practitioners are now appointed and more significantly, Area Courts are under the administrative control of the Chief Judge who is a trained legal practitioner. Secondly, legal practitioners now appear before Area Courts. Thirdly, the appearance of legal practitioners has been a mixed blessing. Legal practitioners 'protect' the interests of litigants, but they have stultified the customary law practice and procedure in the courts and have brought the technicalities of the common law, its attendant delays and high cost of litigation into the Area Court systems.

(a) Qualification of area court judges and control of area courts

One allegation frequently levelled against Area Courts is that the judges manning the courts are generally not well educated. It is also alleged that the minutes of evidence, the records of proceedings and even judgments are written by court clerks or registrars (Oyewo 1999: 81–82). The rules allow this (Area Courts Law, s. 10(1)(b)). However, in none of the Area Courts visited in Ilorin, was this the case. It was the judges that took the minutes of evidence and records of proceedings.

Although only literate persons are now appointed as Area Court judges, controversies on their qualifications remain. Lawyers complain that the courts are not manned by qualified legal practitioners. However, the position is fast changing. Almost all the judges have one form of legal education or another. Many are qualified legal practitioners and others have Diploma Certificates in Law.

One should point out that for customary law there is no specific academic or professional qualification in the country (Oba 2005: 107-108). Even judges of the Customary Court of Appeal and other superior courts are appointed on the basis of their legal qualifications as legal practitioners plus their having "considerable knowledge of and experience in the practice of Customary law" (Constitution, 1999, ss. 266(3), 281(3), 288(2)(b)). For Islamic law, although there are diplomas and certificates in Islamic law, and also combined honours degrees in Islamic law, there is no professional body for Islamic law practitioners. The only known legal requirement under the Constitution in Islamic law is the equally nebulous "recognised certificate from an institution approved by the National Judicial Council", and "considerable experience in the practice of Islamic law" or being "a distinguished scholar of Islamic law" (Constitution, 1999, ss, 261(3), 276(3), 288(2)(a)).

Hitherto, there were no specific qualifications stipulated for Area Court judges, and thus virtually any person could be appointed. Persons with degrees, diplomas and certificates in law have been appointed, and so also have been school certificate holders who had been court registrars for a long time. However, the practice of appointing only legal practitioners who had undergone the common law or the combined common and Islamic law training has taken a firm root in spite of stiff opposition by judges and Kadis who have only Arabic or Islamic studies qualifications (Grand Kadi of Kwara State 2006: xvi). Since 2006, only legal practitioners are appointable as Area Court and Upper Area Court judges (Area Court Law, s. 4A(1)(a), (b), inserted by Kwara State Law Revision (Miscellaneous) (Amendment) Law, 2006). However, judges who are currently serving but are not legal practitioners are allowed to remain until retirement (Area Court Law, s. 4A(2)). It appears that there is now a deliberate policy in the country generally to appoint only legally qualified persons as judges of Area Courts. However, the solving of one problem has intensified the court's crisis of identity.

Area Courts are under the administrative control of legal practitioners. The Kwara State Judicial Service Commission is responsible for the appointment and discipline of Area Court judges in the State (Constitution, 1999, s. 197 and Part II, Third Schedule). The Commission is dominated by legal practitioners with the Grand Kadi as the only representative of Islamic law in the seven-man panel. Islamic law is generally marginalised in the controlling organs of the judiciary in the country (Oba 2004b: 60-62). The Area Courts are under the general supervision of the High Court under the Chief Judge of the State (Area Courts Law, s. 43). This has been a thorny issue. The Kadis argue that the Area Courts should be under the general supervision of the Grand Kadi of the Sharia Court of Appeal (Oba 2004b: 62).

(b) Legal practitioners as counsel in area courts

In 1982, the High Court decided in *Uzodinma v Police* that legal practitioners have a constitutional right of audience in all criminal cases in all courts including Area Courts. In 1984, the Court of Appeal in *Karimatu Yakubu and Anor v Alhaji Yakubu Paiko and Anor* extended this to civil cases. Even though this decision was heavily criticised by scholars such as Tabi'u (1985-1987), Ladan (1993) and Oba (2000a: 127-128), legal practitioners now appear freely in Area Courts and are frequently seen in them. They appear in ordinary business suits without the barrister's wig and gown, which are worn only before superior courts. The Area Courts are not superior courts, being created under section 6(5)(k) of the 1999 Constitution. The judges too appear in flowing traditional robes (*Agbada*) or in simpler long dress (kaftan). A few customary judges are seen wearing western suits.

(c) The impact of legal practitioners on proceedings in area courts

As pointed out earlier, Area Courts have jurisdiction in both customary law and Islamic law matters as well as in English-style statutory criminal law. By their education, legal practitioners are only familiar with English-style common law. They are generally totally ignorant of the rudiments of customary law and Islamic law (Oba 2004a). Yet, these form the overwhelming majority of cases before them. Justice Belgore aptly summarised the pathetic situation of customary courts resulting from the activities of legal practitioners in Area Courts as follows:

> In preparation for the beginning of our constitutional doom, some parts of the country started "renovating" the native courts by putting British trained lawyers as the judges. Instead of quick and just decisions, these customary court judges were only "customary judges" because the law says so, they are not even a cross of customary and common law judges. The courts got worse in matter of delays and ignominious adherence to precedents. In many cases the judges never know the custom of the area they adjudicate upon. The net result is that they employ their personal moral standards on issues of succession, legitimacy, matrimonial causes, custody of children, contracts and other personal laws. (Belgore 1999/2000: 45)

Now, with legal practitioners taking over the customary courts as counsel and judges, the system in the Area Courts is becoming increasing anglicised. Legal practitioners still complain that non-lawyer Area Court judges do not "appreciate" legal points (Odinkalu 1992: 29-32, 87–90). Of course, the judges who are lawyers do. If the system is not overhauled, the common law will sooner or later overwhelm customary law and Islamic law procedures in the Area Courts. They will turn from the distributive justice of customary law to the formal justice of the common law.

(i) Abridgment of customary law evidence and procedure

The tendency is to apply common law rules of evidence and procedure in cases governed by customary law or Islamic law, whereas the law exempts customary and Islamic courts from the ambit of the Evidence Act which codified the rules of the English law of evidence (Evidence Act, s 1(2)(c). See further Oba, 2003: 462-464).

The oath is a prominent means of proof under Customary and Islamic Laws (Oba 2002a). While customary law oaths continue to suffer increasing threats to their recognition in the English style courts or the general courts (Oba 2008a) and their use has declined significantly even in customary courts across the country, the Islamic law oaths are enjoying an increasing relevance and use in the Area and Sharia Courts. The appellate courts, particularly the Sharia Court of Appeal have insisted that the Islamic procedure (which includes Islamic oaths) must be followed strictly in Islamic cases in the Area Courts (Ambali 2003: 95-127; Oba 2005: 162-164). In customary law proceedings, traditional oaths are rarely used, the preferred oath being the common law oath embodied in the Oaths and Affirmations Law. This may be because the Area Courts (Civil Procedure) Rules, 1971 which regulates the Area Courts in civil matters and the Criminal Procedure Code which governs criminal procedure in these courts are patterned closely after the common law civil and criminal procedures respectively. Common law oaths constitute a radical departure from the Islamic and customary law use of oaths (Oba 2002b).

The Area Courts have generally followed Islamic law procedure in Islamic cases[3] but in customary law matters, the English civil law procedure adopted for customary cases by the Area Court (Civil Procedure) Rules 1971 has been followed (Order 11, rules 1-11, Area Court (Civil Procedure) Rules, 1971; Eri 2000: 110-118). Judges and counsel keep making references to these rules and the Criminal Procedure Code. The arguments advanced by counsel generally are also similar to

[3] This is consistent with order 11, Area Court (Civil Procedure) Rules, 1971, which stipulates that Islamic law procedure must be followed in Islamic law matters; see also *Aremu v Akanni* at 13.

those advanced in the English style courts.

(ii) Technicalities

Customary law in indigenous African communities was simple and its administration speedy. The proceedings in Area Courts are supposed to reflect these characteristics. Karibi-Whyte JSC explained the role of Area Courts thus:

> Our new judicial system having accommodated our indigenous system of administration of justice has recognized its informality, malleability to the particular area in which the court exercises jurisdiction, has made provision within the limits of statutory provision enabling them to administer justice as understood by the people and to do substantial justice between the parties before them. Thus what the enabling statutory provisions aim at achieving is the doing of substantial justice in accordance with the native law and custom of the parties before them, any technicality which will stultify the realisation of this objective will be rejected by the court. (See s. 62, Area Courts Edict, 1968). Area Courts are therefore given a wide latitude to enable them do substantial justice. (*Kunso v Udo,* 54)

This is consonant with section 61 of the Area Courts Law which provides:

> No proceeding in an Area Court and no summons, warrant, process, order or decree issued or made thereby shall be varied solely by the reason of want of form but every court or authority established in and for the State and exercising powers of appeal or revision under this Edict shall decide all matters according to substantial justice without undue technicalities.

Karibi-Whyte, JSC, commenting on this provision said:

> It is important to appreciate the fundamental factor that Area Courts created under the Area Courts Edict, 1986 [Benue State] which are the successors of the former native Courts, which in turn were the courts which replaced the pristine traditional methods of the administration of justice are designed to maintain

> and adhere to our indigenous methods of administering justice. (*Kunso v Udo,* 54)

(iii) Delay of cases

Delays in the litigation processes are routine in Nigerian courts. It is not unusual for a case to last several years (Aguda 1986: 13). From the trial court to the Supreme Court, cases have been known to take up to 22 years (as *Ariori v Elemo* did). There are several reasons for this. There are too many cases before the courts. Up to 30 cases are listed before the court daily (Odinkalu 1992: 84). The pattern is still more or less the same in Area Courts in the Ilorin Emirate with as many as 35 cases on the court's docket in some instances. It is simply beyond human capacity to take all the cases listed. Invariably, many are simply adjourned. Legal practitioners too are responsible for some of the delays. They ask for too many adjournments. Again, the common law places a great premium on procedural niceties, rather than on the substantive matter before the court. Hence, there are too many arguments on technicalities that have little or no bearing on the substantive issues in the cases (Oba 1999). The system permits appeals on technical points even when the substantive case is still on. Thus, there can be several interlocutory appeals before a case is eventually concluded by the trial court. These appeals when fortified by orders for stay of proceedings, are responsible for the worst delays within the system. Until the appellate process, which may consist of several steps (to the High Court then to the Court of Appeal and finally to the Supreme Court) determines an interlocutory appeal, a case cannot be brought to a conclusion. There are also the volumes of records of proceedings to be prepared in tens of copies for each appellate stage. The arguments of counsel do much to multiply the records of proceedings.

Secular or Religious Courts?

Area Court judges administering Islamic law generally think of themselves as Qadis in the traditional Islamic sense rather than as the civil servants they are under the law. Although they are not religious courts *de jure*, they are so *de facto*. At least, that is how the judges perceive themselves and that is how the populace perceive them. Since the law they administer, the procedure they follow, and the manner of proof in their courts are based on Islamic law, it is inevitable that they think of themselves as Qadis. The judges frequently cite and rely on Islamic injunctions on judicial ethics. The Sharia Court of Appeal in admonishing an Area Court judge repeated this hadith (a saying of the Prophet Mohammed (SAW):

> Judges are of three categories: two categories will surely go to hell fire while only one will enter paradise. The judge who knows the law and decides in accordance with the law will surely enter paradise. The second is the judge who knows the law but refuses to judge in accordance with the law due to subterranean motive he will enter hell fire. The third judge is one who is not learned in the applicable law but arrogated the power to himself he will surely end up in the hell fire. (Quoted in *Ibrahim v Ibrahim,* 61-62. This hadith is reported in al-Asqalani 1994: 289.)

This is an oft-cited hadith in connection with Muslim judges generally and with Area Court judges in particular. Odinkalu's arguments as to the status of Area Courts though superficially correct, overlook the religious antecedents of the Area Courts (Odinkalu 1992). Their religious flavour remains up to today.

Odinkalu also complained that there was no female judge in the areas covered by his research. This he thinks may be a possible violation of the constitutionally guaranteed rights against discrimination on grounds of sex (Odinkalu 1992: 50). While there are many women among the Magistrates and High Court judges in the Emirate, there is no female judge in any of the Area Courts in the emirate. Nobody can remember if one was ever appointed. This is not strange. Islamic law requires that only males be appointed as judges (Yusuf 1982: 29).

Again, under Islamic law, a non-Muslim cannot be a judge in a court applying Islamic law to Muslims (Ambali 2003: 81). Such a person can however be a judge applying customary law or other religious laws to his own people even within an Islamic State. This is the pattern adopted in Ilorin. All the Area Court judges applying Islamic law are Muslims. There are non-Muslim judges in the Area Courts that administer customary law. Contrary to Odinkalu's assertion, Area Courts when they administer Islamic law have an Islamic flavour. Yet, Area Courts are not really fully fledged Islamic courts. As we have indicated earlier, their judges are public servants whose control and discipline are not in the hands of religious authorities but in the hands of secular public officials. They also deal with criminal laws which are not based on Islamic law. Thus, in many cases, the religious judicial and ethical imperatives are not really relevant in these courts. The circumstances of the court and its judges indicate a serious crisis of identity, not surprisingly, with some very adverse consequences.

Apart from the legal and other procedural consequences, the court's identity crises have aided highhandedness, arbitrariness and corruption in the court. These have given the court a bad reputation among legal practitioners, litigants and the general public.

(a) Highhandedness and arbitrariness

In the past, another serious crisis of identity faced Area Court judges when they were under the direct control of political appointees and they became more or less extensions of politicians.

When the colonial administration took over the running of the alkali courts, the resident was in charge of them. The Native Administration (NA), as the local government was called, succeeded the resident. Between this period and the Area Courts reform of 1967, Area Courts (or the native courts as they were known then), were under local government. During this period, local government officials were elected through partisan politics. Local government officials used the Area Courts to victimise and harass their political opponents (Yahaya 1980: 10–12, 100–101; Mahmud 1988: 29-30). Illegal arrests and undeserved jail sentences were imposed. Judges that refused to cooperate were summarily removed from office. This perverted use of the courts opened them to all sorts of corruption and high-handedness. The Area Courts reform of 1967 removed the Area Courts from the control of politicians, but the high-handedness of the old sometimes surfaces again. A relatively recent example is the case of *Ndache v Nda Yaru* where the Sharia Court of Appeal reprimanded the Area Court for issuing a bench warrant against a party who was absent from court on the day fixed for the hearing of a paternity/custody of child case filed against her.

(b) Corruption

The incidence of corruption was unknown or very low in the pre-colonial alkali era (Ubah 1977: 121). Unfortunately, today corruption is a well-known contemporary problem in Nigeria. Courts generally and Area Courts in particular are not immune. Area Court judges are also frequently accused of trying cases in their houses or in chambers rather than in the open court (Odinkalu 1992: 104-106). It is difficult to get concrete facts but allegations of corruption are common.

Judges in the Ilorin Emirate no longer hold 'court sessions' at home. However, it appears that cases still sometimes proceed informally in the judges' chambers rather than in open court, particularly where there are no legal practitioners in the case. So many persons - litigants, personal visitors, legal practitioners and touts - routinely consult the judges in chambers that one cannot say with complete certainty that none of the visits are made with dubious motives. Some unscrupulous touts, and even legal practitioners, collect money ostensibly for bribing the judge. Such a person then proceeds to the judge's chambers to discuss other things without offering or giving the bribe. He will then upon his return confirm that he had delivered the bribe! It is too easy to have an audience with an Area Court judge in Chambers. It appears that legal practitioners do not observe with rigour the practice whereby the legal practitioner on the other side must be informed and his presence requested before a legal practitioner in the case can discuss any aspect of that case with the judge.[4] It may be that the courts are meant to be informal in the traditional sense, but such solitary visits raise legitimate suspicions.

Another minus for the Area Courts is the presence of touts. Touts are the most oft-complained about features of lower courts in the country. Area Courts are particularly infested with them. There are two types of touts in the Area Courts. There is the 'charge and bail', and there is the *Baba Kekere* (literally in Yoruba 'small father'). The 'charge and bail' basically furnishes bail bond for persons arraigned before Area Courts on criminal charges. Often they act as go-betweens negotiating bribes between accused persons on the one hand and the judge and the police prosecutor on the other hand. *Baba Kekeres* are an exclusive feature of Area Courts throughout northern Nigeria (Yusuf 1982: 42-43). They are not found in superior courts and English-style Courts. They are frequently seen going in and coming out of judges' chambers, and talking with court registrars and clerks. They do not appear in cases except as witnesses. Many believe they specialize in giving false evidence (Yusuf 1982: 42-43). All these show that the ethical tone of the Area Courts has declined remarkably compared to its pre-colonial purely religious-oriented precursors. Touts give the judges a bad image. Attention was drawn to this at a workshop for Area Court judges

[4] It is against the rules for a legal practitioner to discuss a case with a judge in the absence of the legal practitioner on the other side or behave in any way as to create the appearance of gaining special personal consideration or favour from a judge: Rules of Professional Conduct for Legal Practitioners, 2007, rules 30(4),(5), 34. See further Orojo 1979: 57-58.

(Oba 2000). The submission there was that any judge within the vicinity of whose court touts particularly *Baba Kekeres* are present is automatically guilty of corruption. For, if he (the judge) does not tolerate, entertain and welcome their attention, the touts will disappear within a few days, because they would no longer have any reason for hanging around. If the judge keeps his door open to them then they will flourish and collect bribes purportedly or actually on the judge's authority.

Corruption is a general problem in the judiciary. The Justice Eso Panel established in 1983[5] which looked at the problem of corruption in superior courts, that is the High Courts and above, charged over forty judges with corruption. The report was not allowed to see the light of day. There is no Government White Paper on it yet. It is doubtful if there will ever be one. However, the anti-corruption crusade launched by President Obasanjo upon assuming power in 1999 has been a major step in checking corruption in the public service. The Independent Corrupt Practices Commission (ICPC, established by the Corrupt Practices and Related Offences Act, 2000; see Ali 2003) and the Economic and Financial Crimes Commission (EFCC, established by the Economic and Financial Crimes Commission Act, 2002; see Kolawole 2004) established by the administration are putting public officers on their toes. If the momentum is maintained there is no doubt that corruption in all sectors of public life in general and the judiciary in particular, will be greatly reduced if not completely eradicated. Unfortunately, the anti-corruption drive has suffered set backs in recent times under the current Nigerian leadership (Human Rights Watch 2009).

Conflict of law problems: Which law is applicable in particular cases?

Since the 'native law and custom' of Ilorin and the 'prevailing law' in the area is Islamic law, most Area Courts are constituted by single judges learned in Islamic law. The Area Courts in only a few places in the Emirate where customary law is dominant are manned by judges who are experts in customary law. In the remainder of the Emirate, this creates problems for the tiny minority of 'strangers' whose customary law is Yoruba and not Islamic law. No doubt, the volume of work resulting from customary law in these areas does not warrant the establishment of exclusive Area Courts for customary law. Regarding this problem of choice of forum the compromise reached is that such cases are filed at the Upper Area Courts where there are judges learned in customary law. A similar problem

[5] Terms of reference of the Panel, *The Guardian* newspaper, January 10, 1994.

arises for Muslims in the areas where customary law dominates and there are no judges learned in Islamic law in their Area Courts. The usual solution is that such cases are transferred to another Area Court manned by a judge learned in Islamic law.

There is also a problem of conflict of substantive laws between Islamic and customary laws. Personal law matters relating to family law, such as divorce, custody of children and inheritance are the commonest cases in Area Courts. Most of the litigants in the Area Courts are both Muslims and indigenes of the Ilorin Emirate. Yet, conflict of law problems do occur in Area Courts in relation to Muslims. Sometimes, a legal practitioner representing a Muslim litigant would argue that customary law should apply in the case even though all the parties are Muslims and the matter in question relates to personal law (see e.g. *Adisa v Adisa* and comments in Ijaodola 2004). Mostly, however, the problems arise because Muslim litigants complain of the imposition of customary law on them. This is a frequent problem in southern Nigeria where only customary courts and magistrates courts exist (Okunola 1991: 153-156; Olaniyan 2005; Oba 2009). In northern Nigeria, the problem often occurs in places where customary law dominates and the Area Courts are manned by customary law experts. The Sharia Court of Appeal has always firmly resisted this. According to the court:

> The point needs to be made that a Muslim and as long as he or she professes Islam, has no option or choice regarding the application of Islamic law – personal or otherwise onto his person. Having voluntarily assumed the status of a Muslim, he or she is disentitled from accepting or rejecting according to his whims and caprices. He cannot back out therefrom and he must not allow anybody to either encourage or discourage him therefrom. There cannot be a superimposition or juxtaposition of customary law over Islamic law. It cannot be done. It is never done. (*Shittu v Shittu,* 98. See also *Jacob* v *Suleiman*.)

Future of Area Courts: Concluding Observations and Suggestions

Any discussion of the future of Area Courts will necessarily involve a discussion of the future of law in Nigeria. Upon a consideration of the arguments for and against the continued existence of customary law generally (Okany 1984: 223–233) and Area Courts in particular (Mahmud 1988: 28–33), there is no doubt that lower courts at the level of Area Courts will always be needed. The only question is what form they should take. It is doubtful whether the same court, given the current state and content of the lawyer's academic and professional training, can administer concurrently the three types of laws in the country. The Area Courts have tried to do this but they have ended up being 'neither fish nor fowl'.[6] Islamic law proponents see them as common law courts masquerading as Islamic law courts; adherents of the customary law see nothing of their cherished African judicial procedure in the courts; while legal practitioners see them as being largely arbitrary (Odinkalu 1992).

There is a need to clarify the identity and character of Area Courts in the Ilorin Emirate. They are in reality two distinct courts - Islamic and customary courts. They should become separate Islamic and customary law courts respectively while Magistrate courts administer English-style law. This will eliminate the distortions introduced into the administration of these three laws by the present arrangement. It will also meet the yearnings and aspirations of the people who actually want Islamic, customary or English-style laws to govern their affairs respectively. In the case of Islamic law, it also has the added advantage of strengthening the religious flavour of the courts which will be useful in the fight against judicial corruption.

It has been suggested that English-style laws should be administered exclusively by the Magistrate courts, customary law by Customary courts and Islamic law by Sharia courts (Tabi'u 1986; Oba, 2000, 2004a). This is the form pioneered by Plateau State which established Area Courts, Customary Courts and Magistrate Courts to administer the three types of laws respectively. However, the control of these three courts is put in the hands of the Chief Judge of the High Court. At appellate level, the tripartite arrangement continues with appeals from customary law courts going to the Court of Appeal, and those from the Area Courts in matters of Islamic personal law going to the Sharia Court of Appeal while those from the Magistrate courts go to the High Court. This arrangement was adopted with some variations by Zamfara State in 1999. The State abolished Area Courts, created Sharia Courts with exclusive jurisdiction in all Islamic law matters and transferred the customary law jurisdiction of the defunct Area Courts to the Magistrate courts. Under this arrangement, the general supervision of the Area Courts was given to the Grand Kadi as head of the Sharia Court of Appeal, the court to which appeals from Sharia Courts lie, while the Chief Judge supervises the Magistrate courts, appeals from which lie to the High Court. This in our view is the preferred option in places where customary law is not prominent. For the Ilorin Emirate, a tripartite courts system is preferable with the

[6] I am indebted for the phrase 'neither fish nor fowl' to Kumo 1988: 14.

control of the Sharia Courts placed under the Grand Kadi. It is suggested here that in furtherance of this option and its variants, legal education should be fashioned academically and professionally towards separate degrees in common law, Islamic law and customary law respectively. A legal practitioner will then appear in and man only the courts within his area of specialisation.

Others are advocating a fusion of all the courts in the country under an English-style courts system (Agbede 1989: 240–241; Dinakin 1991: 65-68). This is clearly unrealistic because the legal practitioners envisaged as the judges of the unified courts are deficient in learning in customary and Islamic laws. Proponents of this option argue that this could be remedied by reforming legal education so as to accommodate substantial learning in both Islamic law and customary law to the extent that all legal practitioners would be experts in all those laws (Aguda 1988, 1989: 264; Tilley-Gyado 2000: 276-278). This approach is fraught with problems as I have highlighted elsewhere (Oba 2004a: 146). However, it is clear from the arguments of supporters of both parallel and unitary court systems respectively that there is a clear need for a radical review of the curricula at the university and Law School levels in such manner that it should be possible to produce practitioners with standardised academic and professional qualifications in Islamic and customary laws. The options in this regard have been examined in detail elsewhere (Oba 2008b).

Corruption is another problem that must be addressed. As we have seen, corruption is a cankerworm within the Nigerian judicial system. Although the availability of appeals and the firmness of the superior courts have helped check many of the excesses of Area Courts, it is necessary that there is effective machinery for weeding out corrupt judges. However, it is apt to point out that corruption in Nigeria goes far beyond the judiciary, it is a national malaise. It is therefore also necessary that the country undergoes an ethical revolution which will purge the country and its judiciary from corruption.

References

Statutes

(Federal Nigerian statutes unless otherwise stated)

Area Courts (Civil Procedure) Rules, 1971, Cap. A9, *Laws of Kwara State*, 2007.

Area Courts Law, Cap. A9, *Laws of Kwara State*, 2007.
Constitution of the Federal Republic of Nigeria, 1999.
Corrupt Practices and Other Related Offences Act, 2000 (Act No. 5).
Criminal Procedure Code Law, Cap. C23, *Laws of Kwara State*, 2007
Customary Court of Appeal, 1979 (Plateau State).
Economic and Financial Crimes Commission (Establishment) Act, 2002
Evidence Act, Cap. E. 14, *Laws of the Federation of Nigeria*, 2004.
High Court Law, Cap. H2, *Laws of Kwara State*, 2007.
Kwara State Law Revision (Miscellaneous Amendments) Law, 2006.
Oaths and Affirmations Law, Cap. O1, *Laws of Kwara State*, 2007.
Penal Code Law, Cap. P4, *Laws of Kwara State*, 2007.
Rules of Professional Conduct for Legal Practitioners, 2007.

Cases

Adisa v Adisa (2004) *Annual Report Sharia Court of Appeal (Kwara State)* 154.
Aoko v Fagbemi [1961] 1 All NLR 400.
Aremu v Akanni (2002) *Annual Report Sharia Court of Appeal (Kwara State)* 1.
Ariori v Elemo (1983) 1 S.C.N.L.R. 1
Ibrahim v Ibrahim (2003) *Annual Report Sharia Court of Appeal (Kwara State)* 58.
Jacob v *Suleiman* (2005) *Annual Report Sharia Court of Appeal (Kwara State)* 296.
Karimatu Yakubu and Anor v Alhaji Yakubu Paiko and Anor. Sharia Law Reports of Nigeria, Vol. 1 (1961-1989), pp. 126–141
Kubra v Adeoti (1998) *Annual Report Sharia Court of Appeal (Kwara State)* 6.
Kunso v Udo (1990) 2 S.C.N.J. 40.
Madiu v Baba (2006) *Annual Report Sharia Court of Appeal (Kwara State)* 280.
Ndache v Nda Yaru (2005) *Annual Report Sharia Court of Appeal (Kwara State)* 48.
Shittu v Shittu (1998) *Annual Report Sharia Court of Appeal (Kwara State)* 93, 163.
Uzodinma v Police (1982) 3 N.C.L.R. 325.
Usman v Umaru (1992) 7 N.W.L.R. (Pt. 254) 377.

Literature

AGBEDE, I. Olu
1989a 'Legal pluralism: the symbiosis of imported, customary and religious

laws: problems and prospects.' Pp. 235 – 248 in M. Ayo Ajomo (ed.), *Fundamentals of Nigerian Law*. Lagos: Nigerian Institute of Advanced Legal Studies

AGUDA, T. Akinola

1986 *The Crisis of Justice*. Akure: Erese Hills.

1988 *The Challenge for Nigerian Law and the Nigerian Lawyer in the Twenty-First Century* being the Nigerian National Merit Award Winners Lecture delivered on 14 September, 1989, Lagos: Federal Government Press.

1989 'Towards a Nigerian common law.' Pp. 249 – 266 in M. Ayo Ajomo (ed.), *Fundamentals of Nigerian Law*, Lagos: Nigerian Institute of Advanced Legal Studies.

AL-ASQALANI, Hafiz

1994 *Bulugh Marami*. Beirut: Dar al-fikr.

ALI, Yusuf O.

2003 'An overview of the corrupt practices and related offences act, 2000.' *Nigerian Bar Journal* 1/1: 37–70.

ALLOTT, Antony N.

1965 'The Future of African Law.' Pp. 216-240 in Hilda Kuper and Leo Kuper (eds.), *African Law: Adaptation and Development*. Berkeley and Los Angeles: University of California Press.

AMBALI M. A.

2003 *The Practice of Muslim Family Law in Nigeria*. Zaria: Tamaza.

ANDERSON, J.N.D.

1978 *Islamic Law in Africa*. London: Frank Cass.

AYITTEY, G.B.N.

1991 *Indigenous African Institutions*. Ardsley-on-Hudson, New York: Transnational Publishers.

BELGORE, S.M.A.

1999/2000 "Developments in appellate practice in the apex courts" *The Jurist* (Unilorin) 5: 45.

DINAKIN, Yomi.

1991 'The Customary and Sharia Court of Appeal of a State under the 1989 Constitution.' *JUSTICE - a Journal of Contemporary Legal Problems*, 2/1: 63-67.

DOI, Abdur Rahman I.

1990 *Shari'ah: the Islamic Law*. Ibadan: Ikhsan Islamic Publishers. (also London: Ta Ha Publishers, 1984)

ELIAS, Taslim Olawale

1971 'Ilorin land and the land tenure law' *Nigerian Law Journal* 5: 159-161.

ERI, Umaru,

2000 *Comments on Area Courts Law Kogi State of Nigeria.* Kogi State: Enenyo Printing and Publishing.

GRAND KADI OF KWARA STATE

2006 'Speech at the ceremony marking the commencement of the 2006/2007 legal year.' *Annual Report of the Sharia Court of Appeal (Kwara State)*: 10.

HUMAN RIGHTS WATCH

2009 'Letter to Nigerian President Yar'Adua Marking His Two Years in Office' dated 5 June 2009 available at http://www.hrw.org/en/news/2009/06/05/letter-nigerian-president-yaradua-marking-his-two-years-office, accessed 3 September 2009.

IJAODOLA, Rasheed

2004 'Divorcing absentee couple under Islamic law: need for caution' *The Jurist* 9: 147-179.

JIMOH, L.A.K.

1994 *Ilorin: The Journey So Far*. Ilorin: Atoto Press.

KARIBI-WHYTE, A.G.

1993 *History and Sources of Nigerian Criminal Law*. Ibadan: Spectrum Books.

KEAY, E.A. and S.S. RICHARDSON

1966 *The Native and Customary Courts of Nigeria*. London: Sweet and Maxwell.

KOLAWOLE, Adedamola

2004 'An overview of the economic and financial crimes commission act, 2004.' *Nigerian Bar Journal*. 2/1: 131–142.

KUMO, S

1988 'The application of Islamic law in northern Nigeria: problems and prospects.' Pp. 42–51 in Syed Khalid Rashid (ed.), *Islamic Law in Nigeria (Application and Teaching)*. Lagos: Islamic Publications Bureau.

KWARA STATE GOVERNMENT

n.d. *Official Website*. http://www.kwarastate.gov.ng/. Last visited 28 August 2009

LADAN, Muhammed Tawfiq

1993 'Is judicial precedent an Islamic doctrine? *Karimatu Yakubu and Anor v Yakubu Paiko*' *Law in Society* 2:107 - 110

LAST, Murray,

1977 *The Sokoto Caliphate*. London: Longman.

MAHMUD, Abdulmalik Bappa

1988 *A Brief History of the Shari'ah in the Defunct Northern Nigeria*. Jos:

University of Jos Press.

OBA, Abdulmumuni A.

1999 'Attitude to typographical errors in pleadings – technicalities beyond belief: *Eze v Lawal.*' *Calabar Law Journal.* 4/1: 126-135.

2000 *The Due Process of Law and Key Factors in the Application of the Concept in Area Courts.* Paper presented at a Workshop for Area Court Judges from Five States organised by the Nigerian Bar Association, Ilorin Branch and Sponsored by Women, Law and Development, held at Kwara Hotel, Ilorin, 8- 9 June.

2002a '*The* relevance of traditional and Islamic oaths in judicial proceedings in Nigeria.' *UDUS Law Journal* 1/4: 143–161.

2002b *Ascertaining the Veracity of Evidence: A Comparative Study of the Judicial Process in African Law, Islamic Law and Common Law.* Paper presented at the International Conference on Politics, Society and Rights in Traditional Societies: Models and Prescriptions for the Contemporary Nation Building in Nigeria at University of Benin, 16-18 May.

2003 'The shari'ah penal codes and the challenge of the evidence act.' *Nigerian Bar Journal* 1/4: 449-470.

2004a 'Lawyers, legal education and the shari'ah courts in Nigeria.' *Journal Legal of Pluralism* 49: 113–161.

2004b 'Kadis (Judges) of the sharia court of appeal: the problems of identity, relevance, and marginalisation within the Nigerian legal system.' *Journal of Commonwealth Law and Legal Education* 2/2: 49-71.

2005 'The sharia court of appeal: accounting to the public in kwara state.' *The Jurist (University of Ilorin)* 10: 161–168.

2008a 'Juju oaths in customary law arbitration and their legal validity in nigerian courts.' *Journal of African Law* 52: 139–158.

2008b 'Towards rethinking legal education in Nigeria.' *Journal of Commonwealth Law and Legal Education* 6: 97-114

2009 'Complexities and complications in the administration of Islamic and customary laws in Nigeria: *Rabiu v Abasi* (1996) revisited.' *African Journal of Legal Theory* (forthcoming).

OBILADE, A.O.

1998 *Nigerian Legal System.* Ibadan: Spectrum Law Publishing.

ODINKALU, A.C.

1992 *Justice Denied* (*The Area Courts System in the Northern States of Nigeria*). Ibadan: Kraft Books Limited) for Civil Liberties Organisation (CLO).

OKANY, M.C.

1984 *The Role of Customary Courts in Nigeria.* Enugu: Fourth Dimension

Publishers.

OKONKWO, C.O.

1979 *Okonkwo and Naish on Criminal Law in Nigeria*. London: Sweet and Maxwell, second edition.

OKUNOLA, Muri

1991 'Relationship between Islamic law and customary law of succession in southern Nigeria' Pp. 151 - 173 in Yemi Osinbajo and Awa. U. Kalu (eds.), *Towards A Restatement of Nigerian Customary Law*. Lagos: Federal Ministry of Justice.

OLANIYAN, H.A.

2005 'Personal law of succession in south western Nigeria: the dilemma of muslims' *University of Ilorin Law Journal*. 2: 1 – 20.

OROJO, J. Ola

1979 *Conduct and Etiquette for Legal Practitioners*. London: Sweet and Maxwell.

OWOADE, M.A.

1980 'Some aspects of criminal law reform in Nigeria.' *Nigerian Bar Journal* 14: 25.

OYEWO, A.T.

1999 *Issues in African Judicial Process*. Ibadan: Jator Publishing Co.

SAID, Ramadan

1970 *Islamic Law: Its Scope and Equity*. London: privately printed, second edition.

SHAGARI Shehu and Jean BOYD

1978 *Uthman Dan Fodio: the Theory and Practice of his Leadership*. Lagos: Islamic Publications Bureau.

TABI'U, Muhammed

1985–1987 'The right of audience of legal practitioners in shariah courts in Nigeria.' *Journal of Islamic and Comparative Law* 15-17: 17-26.

1986 'Constraints in the Application of Islamic Law in Nigeria.' Pp. 75 - 85 in Syed Khalid Rashid (ed), *Islamic Law in Nigeria (Application and Teaching)*. Lagos: Islamic Publications Bureau.

TILLEY-GYADO, M.

2000 'A Case for the Inclusion of African Customary Law in the Curriculum of Law Faculties in Nigerian Universities.' Pp. 256–257 in I.A. Ayua (ed.), *Nigerian Current Legal Problems, Vols. 2 and 3 (1993–1995)*. Lagos: Nigerian Institute of Advanced Legal Studies.

TSIGA, I.A. and M.A. ADAMU

1997 *Islam and the History of Learning in Katsina*. Ibadan: Spectrum Books

Ltd.

PARK, A.E.W.

1963 *The Sources of Nigerian Law*. Lagos: Africa Universities Press and London: Sweet and Maxwell.

UBAH, C.N.

1982 'Islamic legal system and the westernization process in the Nigerian emirates.' *Journal of Legal Pluralism* 20: 69-93.

1985 *Government and Administration of Kano Emirate 1990-1930*. Nsukka: University of Nigeria Press.

YAHAYA, A.D.,

1980 *The Native Authority System in Northern Nigeria*. Zaria: Ahmadu Bello University Press.

YUSUF, Ahmed Beita

1982 *Nigerian Legal System: Pluralism and Conflict of Laws in the Northern States*. New Delhi: National Publishing House.

FRAGMENTING LAND AND THE LAWS THAT GOVERN IT

Sue Farran

Map of Vanuatu

Source: National Statistics Office, 2004.

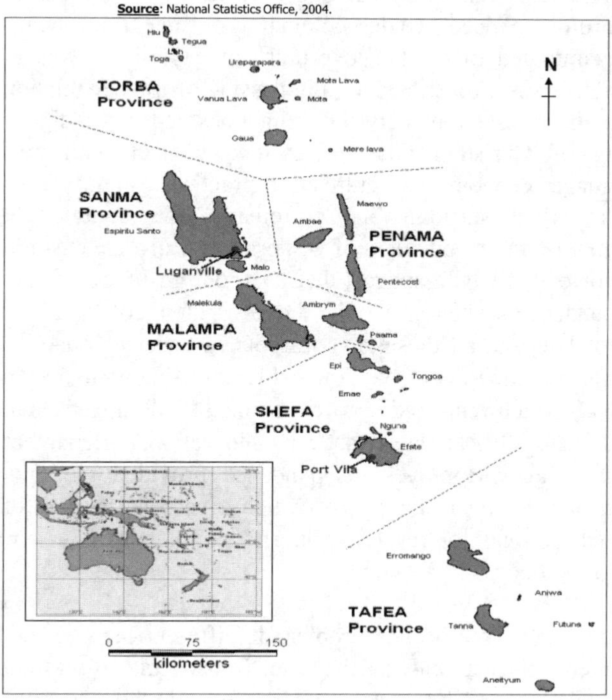

Introduction

The legal pluralism which prevails in many South Pacific islands, especially those of Melanesia, is like an onion, multilayered and changing shape every time one investigates deeper. While the pursuit of understanding may not end in tears, it can certainly be a challenging experience. Take the issue of land tenure in the Republic of Vanuatu.

Prior to contact with outsiders in the late eighteenth and early nineteenth century, the Pacific islanders who inhabited these islands determined their relationship with the land, its resources and the marine environment that surrounded them according to customs and practices which may have been brought with them from elsewhere, or evolved according to need. Under colonial government for many indigenous people customs continued to be the governing force of their lives, although the incursions of English and French agents; the passing of joint regulations to control the relationships and transactions between indigenous and non-indigenous persons; the proselytising of Christian missionaries and contact with new forms of technology, language, economy and cultivation practices, all served to change the wider context in which customs and customary laws operated. There were therefore, even before the introduction of western laws, diverse customs, languages and practices. However I would suggest that legal pluralism really developed as an issue post-independence, when not only did a written constitution become the primary source of law, but all those laws introduced under colonial administration - from France and England under the Anglo-French Condominium government of the New Hebrides - which remained in force, applied to all citizens and residents of Vanuatu, as did, naturally, all laws made by the national parliament as well as existing customary law. Moreover independence provided the opportunity for greater assertion of a national identity, of which a personal system of law is one aspect, and placed the onus for resolving internal conflicts of laws on the national courts and legislative body.

This in itself might not have been a problem if different laws applied to distinct legal subject matters, but that was not the case. In particular it was not the case in respect of land. There are historical reasons for this but the consequence is contemporary. This paper considers the background to this plurality of laws, contemporary manifestations of it, and the advantages and disadvantages of this inner pluralism in the context of development and the recognition or denial of cultural diversity.

FRAGMENTING LAND AND THE LAWS THAT GOVERN IT

Sue Farran

In the hierarchy of laws which apply in Vanuatu the Constitution is supreme and therefore the starting point. The Constitution establishes not only the sources of law to be applied to land, but also the forums for dispute settlement, triggering at the outset a degree of confusion. These forums, however, also provide a key for exploring the plurality which is central to this paper. In particular the evidence presented to support land claims before the islands courts, as reported in the case-law, has been examined to investigate and illustrate the plural nature of customary land tenure.

Land, the law and legal process

The applicable laws

The 1980 independence constitution of the Republic of Vanuatu, restored at one blow perpetual title to all land to the indigenous custom owners (Constitution, Article 74),[1] and provided that the rules of custom should form the basis for the use and ownership of land. No further indication regarding the nature, extent or applicability of the rules of custom was given, and none has been forthcoming, although no doubt this was envisaged. Consequently the 'rules' that govern customary land tenure are inchoate. Nor is any guidance given as to when the observance of custom becomes a 'rule', a point to which I shall return.

Customary tenure however, is not the only form of interest in land. Under colonial influence leases were introduced - originally under French and English laws, and these have been continued post-independence along with more novel forms of land holding such as Strata Title.[2] While perpetual title to land vests in the custom owners, land may be alienated under lease for periods up to seventy-five years, either to other indigenous people, or to non-indigenous people. Once a leasehold is secured over land, then the land can be sub-divided, developed and also used as security for mortgage finance - banks and lenders are reluctant to lend against the

[1] Apart from relatively small areas of public land located in the two metropolitan areas of Port Vila and Luganville.

[2] Freehold estates or absolute ownership was also in use but as it no longer exists is not considered here.

security of land held under customary tenure for a variety of reasons.[3] Inevitably the lease requires that the leaseholder has exclusive possession thereby ousting the claim of the customary owner to use or occupy the land for the duration of the lease - which will span several generations. At the end of the lease the land will in principle revert to the customary owner, but in practice - although in most cases this remains to be tested,[4] the customary owner may have to compensate for improvements or offer to renew the lease.

The formal forums for dispute settlement

The Constitution also made provisions for the establishment of courts which would have - among other things, jurisdiction to determine land claims. Initially it was the Islands Courts with appeal to the Supreme Court that heard land cases. [5] The Island Courts Act (Republic of Vanuatu 2006: Cap 167) conferred power on the Chief Justice to establish such courts throughout the country. The jurisdiction of each court was to be determined by the terms of the Chief Justice's warrant for each court, although the Act envisaged Island Courts having both civil and criminal jurisdiction. They were to be supervised by a chief magistrate but it was the President of the Republic "acting in accordance with the advice of the Judicial Service Commission" who was to appoint "not less than three justices knowledgeable in custom for each Island Court at least one of whom shall be a custom chief residing within the territorial jurisdiction of the court" (s. 3(1)). The court was fully constituted when sitting with three justices and a clerk and the court was to

[3] For example, the lender may be reluctant or unable to come into possession to manage the land and will be unable to sell the land as customary land cannot be alienated. The land could be leased but if it is located in a customary land area this could cause social tensions.

[4] Vanuatu is only a young country so most of these leases still have many years to run.

[5] Island Courts Act 1983, supplemented by the Island Courts (Power of Magistrates) Order 2003; Island Courts (Supervising Magistrates) Rules 2005; Island Courts (Civil Procedure) Rules 2005; Island Courts (Criminal Procedure) Rules 2005; Island Courts (Court Clerks) Rules 2005; Island Courts (Amendment) Act No 29 2006.

> administer the customary law prevailing within the territorial jurisdiction of the court so far as the same is not in conflict with any written law and is not contrary to justice, morality and good order (Island Courts Act, s. 10).

The procedure of these courts was established in subsidiary legislation (Island Courts (Civil Procedure Rules) 1984 as amended). The first courts were set up in 1984 and by 1999 there were eight such courts (Jowitt (1999)). This meant that a number of areas did not have a court to hear disputes relating to customary land. Indeed it has been suggested that

> [t]he most obvious problem is the fact that many of these courts exist in name and warrant only. Adequate funding and personnel are lacking, so most island courts are mere fictions. Those that do operate tend to do so sporadically, resulting in large delays for complainants. (Jowitt (1999)

Although some of these issues have been addressed, it is still the case that there are only eight island courts, which means that many islands, even large ones such as Pentecost, are without a court. Nevertheless, while the applicable law may have been uncertain, the forum and procedure was relatively clear.

However, the jurisdiction of those courts that were established under warrant encompassed not only people from different islands but also observing different customs. This was hardly surprising as

> Vanuatu is very ethnically diverse, with approximately 108 distinct linguistic and cultural groups ... with such cultural diversity there is no such thing as a single custom law that applies to all of Vanuatu.... [A] person may therefore be judged by justices who operate under customary norms that they are not familiar with. (Jowitt (1999)

The courts that did exist were therefore likely to be faced with a plurality of customs informing land tenure practices, and even if those who sat on the bench were knowledgeable in custom it was unlikely that this knowledge could encompass great diversity. The probability of complainants not being satisfied with the adjudication of disputes was therefore, high. Consequently, almost all cases were appealed to the Supreme Court, creating not only an insurmountable backlog of cases, but also subjecting customary land disputes to an adjudication process that was not customary (although assessors knowledgeable in land matters could be asked to assist the bench). Twenty years after independence the Supreme Court refused to hear any more land appeals. In 2001 the civil jurisdiction of island courts to hear customary land disputes was removed (Island Courts (Amendment) Act 2001, which came into effect in 2002).

That same year (2001) the Customary Land Tribunal Act set up a new tier of courts to consider and rule on customary land claims. In part this new structure was designed to address some of the problems identified above. At the lowest level the village tribunal is meant to encompass a particular custom area, so that the chief who chairs it and the two other members co-opted to sit on it (chiefs or elders) are knowledgeable about the custom affecting the land within its jurisdiction - although they are not meant to have a personal interest in the outcome. Where land traverses village boundaries then there is scope for a joint tribunal. Appeals from this local level are to a custom sub-area land tribunal, which represents a larger jurisdictional area in which there may be a number of villages sharing similar customs, and from there to a custom area tribunal and ultimately the island land tribunal. The panels for these tribunals are drawn from chiefs sitting on the area, or sub-area council of chiefs, or island council of chiefs. However, not all areas yet have customary tribunals and the efficiency of those that do exist has been questioned (Republic of Vanuatu Department of Lands 2003). A review of the Customary Land Tribunal system in 2004 found that there were considerable problems including the fact that people were unaware of the tribunals and did not understand how they functioned; there was lack of support for them; and a general lack of ownership of them. Moreover, it was found that the new system was perceived by many chiefs to be undermining customary rules - partly because of the process of appeals and possibility of rehearings (Regenvanu 2008: 65), while in a number of areas disputes about rightful holders of chiefly title raise challenges about the eligibility of those entitled to sit on the tribunals. Further review of the operation of the tribunals is currently underway.

Despite land dispute jurisdiction being transferred to the Customary Land Tribunals, Island Courts continue to hear and rule on land disputes which have been pending prior to the change in the law. Similarly, although apart from the possibility of judicial review or appeal on the grounds of procedural irregularity (exercised in *Umou v Erromango*) the jurisdiction of the Supreme Court over customary land matters ceased, in practice land cases still come before the Supreme Court - and from there to the Court of Appeal, not only on procedural grounds but also because land which is the subject of dispute concerning customary interests may also be subject to leasehold interests or claims.

Under the Land Leases Act (Republic of Vanuatu 2006: Cap 163) only the Supreme Court has jurisdiction to hear disputes concerning leases, pursuant to sections 1 and 100. However, an existing and even registered lease may be affected by a dispute that is pending before the Island Court or Customary Land Tribunal. For example, in the case of *Solomon v Turquoise*, the Court set aside a registered lease because there had been an attempt to register it while there was a title dispute going through the Customary Lands Tribunal. Although the Minister of Lands has statutory power to enter into leases over disputed land, the Supreme Court has held that where he does so ignoring the views of custom owners of which he is aware, then the lease may be held to be defeasible. Similarly, where an existing lease is transferred or sold on, failure to obtain the consent of the custom owners where this is required (for example under Land Leases Act, s. 36), or where there is a dispute between custom owners as to whether the lease should be sold on or not (see for example *Vanuatu Fisaman Cooperative Marketing Consumer society Ltd v Jed Land Holdings*), could lead to the subsequent lease being ruled invalid, especially if the original lease was granted in breach of the required consents.[6] Magistrates courts too may encounter land disputes in the course of dealing with other related matters, for example family issues concerning succession, legitimacy and beneficial entitlement to income generated by land.

There is therefore a plurality of formal forums for determining land issues.

Informal forums

To complicate matters further however, besides these formal forums for hearing

[6] It is not entirely clear if this is mandatory as the section reads:

> Upon the registration of a lease containing an agreement by the lessee that he will not dispose of the land leased or any part thereof or interest comprised therein without the written consent of the lessor, the agreement shall be noted in the register of the lease, and no dealing with the lease shall be registered until the written consent of the lessor verified in accordance with section 78 has been produced to the Director.

land disputes there are also informal forums held at the village or family level, where a single chief or a committee may hear land matters and adjudicate these, usually with the aim of arriving at a negotiated settlement, maintaining the peace and harmony of a village or local area or arriving at an equitable distribution of resources. This traditional process of resolving land disputes pre-dates independence and seems to have survived the Anglo-French Condominium - except where such disputes were between indigenous and non-indigenous land users and occupiers.[7] For many people these local forums are the only ones to which they have access. The contemporary role and function of chiefs within this legal system is unclear. On the one hand, at a national level, the Constitution states that the National Council of Chiefs

> has a general competence to discuss all matters relating to custom and tradition and may make recommendations for the preservation and promotion of ni-Vanuatu culture and languages (Constitution, Article 30(1)).

(It also has the right to "be consulted on any question, particularly any question relating to tradition and custom, in connection with any bill before Parliament" (Constitution, Article 30(1)). It appears, although it does not say so, that this includes making statements of policy on land or customs regarding land, as these policy statements are referred to by Island Courts from time to time (see for example *Awop v Lapenmal*). However, the National Council of Chiefs (Organisation) Act (Republic of Vanuatu 2006: Cap 183), says nothing about their powers, dealing only with the composition of the Council. Under the more recent National Council of Chiefs Act 2006, the functions of Island and Urban Council of Chiefs are stated. These are to: resolve disputes according to local custom; prescribe the value of exchange of gift for a custom marriage; to promote and encourage the use of custom and culture; to promote peace, stability and harmony, and to promote and encourage sustainable social and economic development (s. 13). On the other hand, none of the above provisions appear to give Councils of Chiefs at national, local or village level adjudicative powers as such. Nor is it clear where chiefs who do not sit on these various councils, fit in. In a number of reported Island Court decisions reference is made to informal dispute resolutions and the decisions of chiefs, but these do not invariably determine the outcome any

[7] In such cases British and French agents seem to have intervened, at least until the Joint Court was established under the Condominium government under the 1906 Convention.

more that written documents are taken as *prima facie* evidence of title or transactions.

Moreover chiefs have a number of roles. They are not merely the adjudicators of disputes. They also hold and often control interests in land which in a hierarchical social structure may confer considerable power on them as well as obligations. Indeed it may be difficult to disassociate chiefly title from customary land tenure. It has been held that

> [t]his chiefly system is attached or twined with the land tenure system ... [because] a chief once ordained by his paramount chief is always allotted a land to work. In return, such head chief must perform custom leases to the paramount chief or other subordinate chiefs who had allocated them Land" (*Mata v Mata,* referring to the custom of Tonga, Shepherds and North Efate).

Moreover, in some parts of Vanuatu, such as north-west Malekula, rank and land rights are hierarchal, with a paramount chief granting land within his land to lesser chiefs who in turn grant land to others within his bloodline. The paramount chief is responsible for ensuring that everyone within the territory he governs has land and for distributing it equally to subordinate chiefs (*Sanhabat v Salemunu*). However in Ambrym it is clear that while the person who originally settled on the land and exerted control over it was likely to become the paramount or senior chief,

> [t]he community as a whole would have other chiefs beside the land owning chief. A chief would normally be nominated by the community based on wealth, bravery and other common characteristics. The land owning unit would also have a chief, a nakamal and a nasara. There would be other chiefs as well within his controlled land. (*Welwel v Family Rorrmal*)

As these chiefs progress up the hierarchy of chiefly titles through pig-killing ceremonies so their power and influence can increase, but equally it can be challenged, for example if they loose popular support. Chiefs today, moreover, may combine political power with traditional power, or assert their authority on the basis of preferment conferred under colonial administration – which often misinterpreted the traditional social organisation of indigenous societies.

The ambiguous role of chiefs, as both figures of authority, adjudicators of disputes and customary land owners is further complicated by the fact that disputed titles are heard by the Island Courts, while land claims are heard by the Customary Land Tribunals. The competence of chiefs to adjudicate land claims within and outside the formal system has been challenged (Mackenzie 2006: 4), and the possibility of transferring from an informal system to the more formal one of the Customary Land Tribunal - in which the same chief(s) may sit, means that disputes can continue over an extended period of time. Nor should it be overlooked that judges in the formal courts may claim familiarity with custom that they bring to bear in non-customary courts, or may claim a familiarity with custom that might be questionable, at the very least on the grounds that they are seeing that custom as an outsider, or through translation, or through the lens of a person educated in a different system.

There are therefore not only many forums, but also many possible adjudicators. Added to this there are also many laws, if customs have the force of law. It is to the evidence of these customs that this paper now turns.

Customary land tenure

Traditionally the writings of anthropologists have provided an insight into customary land holding patterns and practices. (For more detailed comment on customary land tenure in Vanuatu see: Guiart 1996; Rodman 1995.) For the lawyer, however, the reported decisions of local courts provide a rich repository of information relating to land claims, in which can be traced some of the earliest land alienation to colonial settlers and missionaries right up to the present day alienation and sub-division of land to developers, as well as changes in use from subsistence agriculture to tourism entrepreneurship. Indeed the evidence led to support or refute indigenous claims to land may provide insight into past and present customary laws, although they tend to be claims of fact or opinion rather than law. In particular, free from the rules of procedure and evidence that constrain the more formal court system, these case studies reflect value systems in a shifting environment, where the claims of custom must work alongside bills of rights in written constitutions and the provisions of international conventions without losing its way. Although not presented as rules, the process of creating law reports may itself be seen as shaping and articulating customary law by converting oral histories into written records for future generations. So, while the recording of land disputes in writing is one way of ensuring that customs and customary forms of land tenure are not lost, at the same time this process changes custom, not only in form, but also in substance.

The Nature of Indigenous Land Tenure in Vanuatu

As indicated, customs are not presented as a set of rules or principles in the reported cases but as evidence of fact. The two main types of evidence that tend to be offered in land disputes are evidence of boundary descriptions and evidence of genealogies. Boundary descriptions involve tracing the physical boundaries of land by reference to physical objects, such as paths, streams, trees rocks, rivers, and later gates, roads, fences, airstrips, schools, churches etc. Names given to places - especially in the local language, are also significant, as is the ability to identify them on a site visit. These visits are required by law in the case of land claims (Rule 9). To the outsider, evidence of bloodlines are extremely complex and often confused by factors such as custom and baptismal names applying to the same person, or an accumulation of names over the course of a lifetime through the acquisition of titles through grade-taking; polygamy; adoption and the misspelling of names when committed to writing. It also clear that genealogies can be manipulated and selectively created to achieve desired outcomes. These problems may be so pervasive that the court is unable to reach a conclusion, as happened for example in *Billy v Ameara*, in a dispute that had been pending for twenty years. Challenges on the grounds of falsified or fabricated family trees are common. Genealogies will often need to be corroborated by supporting genealogies, or may be undermined by challenging the number of generations recalled or weaknesses in related evidence such as custom ceremonies linked to awards of status, or claims to long histories which are not supported by physical evidence - for example the number or size of stones used to mark pig-killing rituals.

The link between claims of fact and the emergence of custom rules arises when the court has to decide what weight to give to the evidence. Something is deemed to be a custom carrying authority when it amounts to a

> *rule blong law we ifomem fasin mo conduct blong pipol long wan society we hemi establish bifo finis mo ino replacem any kastom. Law ia oli no writem daon mo pipol iliv wetem.* [A long-standing legal rule which determines the way in which people of a society conduct themselves and act, which informs but does not replace custom. Such a law is not written down but lived]. (*Tenene v Kalmarie*)

In the Shepherd Islands a customary obligation is similarly defined as "an existing principle which informs/shapes the way in which the people in one society conduct themselves and on which customs are based. The rule/principle is unwritten but people live according to them" (*Mata v Mata)*.

Although, as is common in Melanesia, the customs relating to land are not homogenous, there are similarities which emerge though the case-law. Indeed claims of difference may be over emphasised - possibly for other reasons.[8] Traditionally rights to land were created by settling on the land and building the first '*nasara*' or meeting place there.[9] Subsequently title could be established

[8] For example, to distinguish political allegiances to different 'Big Men' or to ensure that marriage is to those within or outside a particular clan depending on what rules prevail in any one area.

[9] 'Nasara' – dancing ground or public area in a village (Crowley 1995: 165). See for example *Manassah v Koko* in which it was explained, with reference to land tenure in Malekula, that

> [i]n this region, land is communally owned based on common descent, residence within a nasara and participation in common activities. A tribe or a bloodline is identified with the land through its nasaras . Within an original or big nasara there are small nasaras or *Smol faea* which are associated in some respect with the original nasara and its paramount chief. The same word *smol faea* is interchangeably used for referring to a subordinate or lower chief. The same token is applied with the word *Big faea* meaning higher chief. Individuals within a tribe are closely tied up with his territory by affinity and consanguinity through blood and marriage.

Similarly in Paama it was stated:

> [G]enerally the island of Paama is predominantly a patrilineal society. Ownership of customary land is communal or collectively owned based on common descent, residence within a nasara and participation in common activities. A tribe or bloodline is identified with the land through the nasaras. Individuals within the clan are closely tied up with their territory by affinity and consanguinity through blood and marriage. A group of persons

through the physical evidence of graves, boundary markers, the planting of trees, and oral evidence of lineage and certain ceremonies.[10] In some cases people from one island were allowed to settle on land in another island, either because of established blood or affinity links or as licencees fleeing disaster or fighting on their home island. These migrants came under the guardianship of the custom land owners. The transfer of land from one generation to the next was, in some areas, matrilineal, and in others patrilineal. Sometimes it would change from one system to the other, and then back again, or be ambi-lineal. Tracing genealogies therefore was, and still is, an important aspect of land claims and often contentious. Similarly there may be differences in interpreting the applicable custom.

At the same time, consideration of the case-law reveals much about the various facets that make up customary land tenure, including: cosmology and rituals that inform human associations with land; the importance of ancestors and kinship structures; the significance of physical features; and the importance of oral history. So for example, from the reported cases of the Island Courts we learn that the custom in Tongoa, Shepherd Islands and parts of North Efate is that where a paramount chief grants land to use to a lesser chief, the latter must

> ... perform custom leases to the paramount chief or other subordinate chiefs who had allocated them Land. There are two types of custom leases namely *'Fanga Sokora'* (first harvest of vegetables) and *'Nasau Tonga'* (harvest of animal) paid to the chief. This is a customary obligation that is practiced from generations to generation throughout the Shepherd Islands. (*Mata v Mata*)

Similarly in Epi

> ... there is a customary obligation for a Paramount Chief to allocate land to his assistants together with their boundary limits.

> belong to a family line and a territory is sometimes identified with a totem, such as a plant or an animal. (*Holuon v Edward)*

[10] For example where pig-killing is the standard custom ritual for ascending through the ranks of chief stones may be used to mark pig-killing sites (*Sanhabat v Salemunu*). Customs to do with marriage, adoption and burial are also frequently recalled.

> As a matter of reciprocity a custom lease is normally paid to the paramount Chief. .. any isolation or absence of these founding aspects to land would prove an invalid custom. (*Family Mokono v Peter*)[11]

In central Malekula the case law demonstrates that the communal ownership of land is based on three elements: "common descent, residence within a nasara and participation in common activities". Individual rights are dependent on a person's association with a tribe or a bloodline – through affinity or consanguinity, which in turn is "identified with the land through their nasaras" (*Alanson v Malingmen*, confirmed in *Sanhabat v Salemunu*). Patrilineal inheritance through the eldest son predominates. However the eldest son is expected to provide for equal distribution between his siblings. (A similar obligation is found in parts of Santo: *Noel v Toto.)* Matrilineal inheritance only comes into play if there are no male heirs and then only as an interim measure (*Abel v Timothy*. Note however that 'interim' may span several generations.) However, there are "customary obligations that requires strict performances in order that the right to own the land can be transferred to the mother's children". These are explained thus:

> ... the mother's line ... is under customary obligations to provide some genre of customs gifts or payment of recognition to the patrilineal line. Such sort of ritual would in return allow and guarantee the children of the mother having blood connection to the patrilineal line to secure some rights of use of the land of their male heirs. (*Tomoyan v Shem)*

Anyone adopted into a bloodline has a lesser right than a natural member of that bloodline: "adoption is only a sign of acceptance to live under the guardianship of another family ... this acceptance or recognition would only exten(d) to the right to use the land excluding ownership" (*Alanson v Malingmen)*.[12]

---

[11] The use of the word 'lease' here is confusing. A 'tithe' or 'tribute' might be more appropriate.

[12] This is distinguishable from the view of the National Council of Chiefs – the Malvatumauri which suggests that adoption after a period of four or six generations would confer full rights of ownership. In central Malekula this would only be the case if there were no bloodline male heirs.

While Malekula has two main tribes 'Big Nambas' and Smol Nambas' there are variations in customs within these. For instance in one case it is explained that

> ... the custom practiced in this locality varies from that habitually observed by the smol nambas tribe in the central part of the island of Malekula. A nasara is divided into three nakamals. It is often described in the following words: "A nasara is like a house which has three main parts, the front, the body and the back or tail". Authority or respect is always paid to the head or front of the mansion. The head of the house or nasara is traditionally called *(Amai)*, the body (*Amahai*) and the tail *(Amesuwe)*. (*Kaising v Kaites)*

In south Pentecost, where settlers and missionaries caused people to relocate within the island, it appears that land use and ownership rights may be acquired not only by bloodlines but through the appropriate performance of custom ceremonies, for example pig killing, observing funeral duties and rituals, and ensuring that infant children are reared on the land (*Tabi v Tabisari:* in this case it was held that land could pass through both sides of the family). Similarly in Ambrym it has been explained that

> ownership of customary land is communal or collectively owned based on common descent, residence within a nasara and participation in common activities. A tribe or bloodline is identified with the land through the nasaras. Individuals within the clan are closely tied up with their territory by affinity and consanguinity through blood and marriage. A group of persons belong to a family line and a territory is sometimes identified with a totem, such as a plant or an animal. (*Welwel v Family Roromal*)

Totem associations are also found in South Efate.

Fragmenting the land

Cases brought before the courts and tribunals reveal the multiplicity of interests over land that can exist in custom and which have co-existed over many generations. Sometimes it is this multiplicity of traditional interests which cause disputes, and often these are resolved in traditional ways. In recent years however, tension is more likely to arise because those who claim to be the custom owners are seeking to develop the land or negotiate with investors for a lease (for example, *Malas v Tretham Construction Ltd)*, and seeking to exclude thereby, the non-ownership rights and interest of others. The nature of land use is therefore changing the cause of disputes. This potential for disputes is aggravated by a number of factors. These include the power of the Minister of Lands to intervene to manage land where ownership is in dispute, the growth of individualism whereby group interests may be sacrificed for individual gain and advancement, a largely unregulated market populated by middlemen which encourages and brokers land alienation and land acquisition between indigenous and non-indigenous parties, and pressure by external agencies for Vanuatu to develop its opportunities for inward investment, to capitalise its limited resources and put in place frameworks which promote economic development, often at the cost of sustainability.

Not only is the climate and environment of land transactions and land use changing. The procedure of dispute settlement is also changing the way in which land interests are presented and perceived.

Despite the modification of rules of evidence, indicated above; the exclusion of legal representation; and the expectation that those who sit to hear customary land claims are knowledgeable about custom, it seems inevitable that committing the record of the court or tribunal deliberations to writing will change customary land tenure, distinguishing oral custom which has not been subject to court or tribunal scrutiny, from that which has. This will give rise to a duality of custom: the recorded and the unrecorded.

Once there is a written record then there is the possibility that this will be referred to in future cases, partly due to the rule of precedent which informs the jurisprudence of the courts in common-law-influenced systems, and also because similar fact cases will lend themselves to recollected former decisions. In this way previously oral evidence may become frozen in time, codified, and less adaptable to changed or changing circumstances. The development of certainties through case-law is part of the common-law mind-set, which dislikes in particular uncertainty as to ownership of property, the idea of land lying waste or idle, or the possibility that a case once decided upon, could be reopened by subsequent parties. Evidence of this process can be found in some of the more recent judgments of the Malekula Island Court, where the narration of 'the Law, Custom and History' is being repeated almost verbatim from previous cases even where the land is situated in different places and the history and customs are different.

The language of the court may also change custom. Court proceedings are in Bislama, one of the three official languages of the Republic of Vanuatu. Where a witness or claimant does not speak Bislama then an interpreter may be used. The language of the court record however may be in English or Bislama (or potentially French). However the languages of education are English or French, so the ability to write Bislama tends to be learned informally - with consequent variations in spelling. Moreover legal language or concepts may be adopted.[13] In some cases this has a significant effect on the application of customary practice. For example in *Awop v Lepenmal*, consideration of the Convention for the Elimination of All Forms of Discrimination Against Women (CEDAW),[14] read with the written provisions of the Constitution (Article 5(1), led to the court holding that advancing the traditional superiority of land claims based on patrilineal descent and affiliation over matrilineal ones was discriminatory, despite the fact that the claim being sought was a historical one, not a contemporary one, thereby distinguishing it on the facts from the case of *Noel v Toto*, which was referred to. A similar line of reasoning was followed to support a matrilinially based claim in *Haitong v Tavulai Community*. Similarly in the latter case, evidence was led that indicated land had been taken by force and settled on by the victors, who later alienated some of it to foreigners. The court held that not only was the idea that land taken in battle became the victors contrary to customary practice, but also that "[t]his is a selfish idea and cannot find favour in this modern world with laws upholding principles of natural justice, fairness and equality" (*Haitong v Tavulai Community*). Consequently even land obtained by conquest had to be returned to the original owners - even where these had been decimated or scattered by the tribal warfare. Arguably this retrospective application of contemporary legal principles to fact based claims of historical events is inappropriate and was not intended under the provisions of the Constitution. This approach may also be inconsistent with the fundamental meaning of custom, indicated above, but also marks a departure from earlier case law where it was made clear to the parties that:

[13] For example the expression 'time immemorial' was used in *Awop v Lapenmal*, while the transfer of land as a consequence of a bet was rejected in *Haitong v Tavulai Community* on the grounds that it had not been made in 'a goodwill manner' and was not a 'legitimate' or 'binding' agreement.

[14] This was integrated into domestic law by the Convention on the Elimination on Discrimination Against Women by the Ratification Act of Parliament No. 3 of 1995.

> *Kot imas mekem iklia long ol patis se ol storian we bae oli talem long Kot blong pruvum se whu nao iraet ona blong graon ia bae kam aot nomo long ol kastom blong yumi long Efate mo Pango. Hemia imin se ol patis oli no save tokbaot loa blong waetman blong pruvum kes blong olgeta. Oli mas tokbaot nomo wanem we kastom italem se olgeta nao oli tru kastom ona long graon ia*' [The court must make it clear to all the parties that the stories they narrate to support their claim to the land must derive from the customs of this place. That means that the parties must not talk about or rely on white man's law to support their claim, but only the true custom of this area. (My translation)]. (*Kalmatalu v Wit*. See similarly *Family Mermer v Taliban*.)

As the value of land as a marketable commodity increases, so it is likely that more litigation will ensue and while representation by lawyers before the customary land tribunals is not permitted by the legislation, it is highly probably that those who can afford to will seek professional or quasi-professional assistance. The language of the law will then creep in and it too will change concepts and meanings.

Conclusion: Development and the Recognition or Denial of Cultural Diversity

This plurality of laws which may apply, forums which may be seized and procedures which may be followed are seen by some as an obstacle to development. In particular they are seen as inhibiting the commoditisation of land for which clarity of ownership and indefeasibility of title is desirable. For example, the 2006 *Final Report of the National Land Summit* states in respect of the identification of legitimate custom land owners, that one of the problems was that there were "no clear custom rules available for chiefs to go by" (Tahi 2006: 24). Similarly writing about the land tenure system of South Efate, Fingleton et al. have stated "there is confusion about what is customary and how far kastom can form the basis for modern land tenure" (Fingleton et al. 2008: 29). At the same time however, this complex plurality of land interests may operate as a bulwark against too rapid land alienation. Both sides may lay claim to the obscure and elusive nature of customary land tenure – versus the certainty of introduced land interests and estates such as lease, freehold, registered title and surveyor's maps. In an arena where there is little equality of bargaining power, and where developers are likely to have financial and legal resources, the confusion of customary land tenure may operate to protect indigenous interests. This may of course be a charade, a masque. For while there is a plurality of customs which determine land interests, a reading of the case-law suggests that this plurality is not indecipherable, unknown or uncertain, except where a party who desires it to be so makes it so. Maintaining a pluralism within pluralism may be, either consciously or unconsciously, a way of maintaining indigenous integrity and cultural diversity against the onslaught of globalisation and universalism; a way of frustrating the fragmentation of land that is alien to and often in conflict with, the fragmentation that takes place in custom, especially when the emphasis is on individualism and monetary economies and ignores the need for inter-generational equitable distribution of land and its resources and the importance of social cohesion and community support in a country where the state provides virtually no social welfare of security. Pluralism within pluralism may therefore be not just a shield, but a sword.

References

Cases

(Citations to cases are to the reports at http://www.paclii.org/vu/cases/VUIC/)

Abel v Timothy [2005] VUIC 5.
Alanson v Malingmen [2004] VUIC 2.
Awop v Lapenmal [2007] VUIC 2.
Billy v Ameara [2004] VUIC 3.
Family Mermer v Taliban [2003] VUICB 2
Family Mokono v Peter [2003] VUIC 2.
Haitong v Tavulai Community [2007] VUIC 3
Holuon v Edward [2007] VUIC 4.
Kaising v Kaites [2006] VUIC 1.
Kalmatalu v Wit [2003] VUICB 3.
Malas v Tretham Construction Ltd [1995] VUIC 1.
Manassah v Koko [2005] VUIC 3
Mata v Mata [2003] VUIC 1.
Noel v Toto [1995] VUSC 3.
Sanhabat v Salemunu [2005] VUIC 6.
Solomon v Turquoise [2008] VUSC 64.

Tabi v Tabisari [2004] VUIC 5
Tenene v Kalmarie [2004] VUICB 1.
Tomoyan v Shem [2007] VUIC 1.
Umou v Erromango [2008] VUSC 65.
Vanuatu Fisaman Cooperative Marketing Consumer society Ltd v Jed Land Holdings [2008] VUSC 73.
Welwel v Family Rorrmal [2007] VUIC 5.

Literature

CROWLEY, Terry
1995 *A New Bislama Dictionary*. Suva: Institute of Pacific Studies.
FINGLETON, Jim, Anna NAUPA and Chris BALLARD
2008 'Village Land Trusts in Vanuatu: 'One Common Basket.' Pp. 21-45 in Australian Agency for International Development, *Making Land Work, Vol. 2, Case Studies on customary land and development in the Pacific*. Canberra: Government of Australia. Available from http://www.ausaid.gov.au/publications.
GUIART, Jean
1996 'Land Tenure and Hierarchies in Eastern Melanesia.' *Pacific Studies* 19: 1-30.
JOWITT, Anita
1999 'Island courts in Vanuatu.' *Journal of South Pacific Law* Working Paper 3. Available at http://www.paclii.org/journals/fJSPL/vol03/
MACKENZIE, Debra
2006 'Case note: *Valele Family v Touru* [2002] VUCA 3: The legality of customary land disputes in Vanuatu.' *Journal of South Pacific Law* 10(2). Available at http://www.paclii.org/journals/fJSPL/vol10no2/7.shtml.
REGENVANU, Ralph
2008 'Issues with Land Reform in Vanuatu.' *Journal of South Pacific Law* 12(1):63-67. Available at http://www.paclii.org/journals/fJSPL/vol12no1/
REPUBLIC OF VANUATU
2006 *Laws of the Republic of Vanuatu – Consolidated Edition 2006*. Available at http://www.paclii.org/vu/legis/consol_act/
REPUBLIC OF VANUATU DEPARTMENT OF LANDS
2003 *Land Tribunal Progressive Report*. Ref No: LD:/AHKM/ahkm. December 12. Port Vila.

RODMAN, Margaret
1995 'Breathing Spaces: Customary Land Tenure in Vanuatu.' Pp. 65-108 in R. Gerard Ward and Elizabeth Kingdon (eds), *Land, Custom and Practice in the South Pacific*. Cambridge: Cambridge University Press.

TAHI, Stephen
2006 *Final Report: National Land Summit*. Port Vila: Government of the Republic of Vanuatu.

BOOK REVIEW

Franz von Benda-Beckmann, Keebet von Benda-Beckmann, and Anne Griffiths (eds), *The Power of Law in a Transnational World: Anthropological Enquiries*. Oxford/New York: Berghahn Books. 2009. 280 pp.

Ralph Grillo

This collection is the second in a series stemming from conferences organised by the Edinburgh School of Law and the Max Planck Institute for Social Anthropology, Halle, Germany; the first, *Mobile People, Mobile Law*, appeared in 2005, published by Ashgate (Benda-Beckmann et al. 2005). Like the earlier book, the present volume attests to the vitality of the intellectual links between anthropologists, lawyers, political scientists and others in the sociological study of law (in the broadest sense) in contemporary societies. Thus it may be profitably read alongside other collections that have appeared recently such as Mehdi et al eds. *Law and Religion in Multicultural Societies* (Mehdi et al. 2008), or Foblets and Renteln eds. *Multicultural Jurisprudence* (Foblets and Renteln 2009), as well Ayelet Shachar's monograph, *Multicultural Jurisdictions (*Shachar 2001), or Werner Menski's *Comparative Law in a Global Context* (Menski 2006). Certainly the book has much of interest for readers of the present journal which has over many years contributed significantly to defining what is now a burgeoning field.

Following a helpful introduction by the editors, the volume is divided into three sections on 'Power of Law as Discourse: Claims to Legitimacy and Higher Morality', 'The Intersection of Legalities', and 'Religion as a Resource in Legal Pluralism'. The ethnographic scope is wide with chapters on Scotland, Burundi, Indonesia and Bhutan, as well as North America, and there is considerable diversity in subject matter including Islamic and civil courts, fisheries management, development projects and children's courts. This may make it sound more eclectic than it is, as there is much common ground between the contributors and the variety of contexts and situations are valuable for showing how the unifying themes described briefly above work out on different grounds. Rather than going over each chapter in detail, this review reflects more generally on the field within which the volume is situated and the contribution it makes to it.

The subtitle is 'Anthropological Enquiries', and most though not all the contributors are indeed anthropologists. The relationship between anthropology and the law has a long history which can be traced at least to the 19th century. It flourished in Britain and the United States in the 1940s and 1950s with important work, *inter alia*, on Native Americans and the peoples of sub-Saharan Africa. These were colonial or quasi-colonial contexts in which systems of 'customary' and ruling 'state' law co-existed or came into conflict, especially under conditions of 'indirect rule'. The work of Max Gluckman was, of course, most notable in that regard, but he was far from alone. Over some 30-40 years, however, and despite the efforts of luminaries such as Laura Nader (who makes a telling contribution to the present volume) or Lawrence Rosen, legal anthropology lost salience. This is not to say that it disappeared or that the situations in which it had earlier flourished diminished in significance, but for a long while it lost its place in the mainstream of the discipline, which it regained only in the present century.

There were several reasons for its re-emergence: the awakening by anthropologists to the growing international significance of conventions of human rights and their impact in situations which they study; increasing attention to multicultural societies in which populations of immigrants and settlers of migrant origin make claims on legal systems, notably but not only in Europe and North America, claims which sometimes appear to conflict with human rights as defined by international conventions; the rise of Islam and the global importance of Islamic law, or demands for the implementation of Islamic law; continuing and indeed increasing attempts by many post-colonial societies to align the law and legal practice with 'traditional' values; and finally, the legal implications of the 'war on terror' and its effect on societies and peoples many anthropologists study. While there is nothing in the present volume on the law and multiculturalism in the North (though the chapter on Scottish children's courts by Anne Griffiths and Randy Kandel has relevance for multicultural themes explored elsewhere) the chapters reveal the significance of these developments for contemporary students of anthropology and other disciplines.

The particular contribution of this volume to the debates to which studies such as those mentioned above are helping to shape, is first, as its title implies, a concern with law and power, and with the law as a site within which power relations are articulated and expressed, and through which hegemony may be confirmed, or sometimes denied. Secondly, the situations within which such struggles are located are here principally ones in which there is a multiplicity of norms, values and legal forms; that is the terrain is constituted by legal and other pluralisms. Thirdly, the studies are firmly contextualized and where comparisons are made similarities and differences are rigorously located in their appropriate context. Fourthly, as does other recent work, many of the contributions break with the 'methodological nationalism', as Wimmer and Glick Schiller called it, which has traditionally characterised the Western lawyer's conception of the law. Fifthly, and consistent with that, there is much emphasis on the analysis of discourse *about* the law, which is often international and transnational, with several contributors taking an approach which might be described as 'discursive ethnography', discourse viewed ethnographically. This is apparent in both the early chapters concerning debates about human rights and recent anti-terror legislation, and in the final section, for example the chapter by Richard Whitecross analysing the 'buddhicization' of the courts and legal practices in Bhutan.

That said, it has to be admitted that it is occasionally difficult to see why some chapters qualify as legal anthropology, except by expanding the scope of the notion of the 'legal' in unacceptably loose ways, or at least in ways which ought to be rigorously controlled. While it is entirely legitimate and indeed important to encompass people and institutions operating 'in the shadow of the law', there is always the danger that anything becomes 'law', and thus law becomes nothing. Anthropologists are particularly prone to dissolving distinctions, and often it is important to do so, but it may sometimes lead to a kind of 'ethnographic solipsism' which has to be avoided.

References

BENDA-BECKMANN, F. von, K. von BENDA-BECKMANN and Ann GRIFFITHS (eds.)
2005 *Mobile People, Mobile Law: Expanding Legal Relations in a Contracting World*. Aldershot: Ashgate.
FOBLETS, Marie-Claire and Alison Dundes RENTELN (eds.)
2009 *Multicultural Jurisprudence: Comparative Perspectives on the Cultural Defense,* Oxford and Portland Oregon: Hart Publishing.
MEHDI, Rubya, Hanne PETERSEN, Erik SAND and Gordon WOODMAN (eds.)
2008 *Law and Religion in Multicultural Societies*, Copenhagen: DJØF Publishing,
MENSKI, Werner
2006 *Comparative Law in a Global Context: The Legal Systems of Asia and*

Africa (2nd ed.). Cambridge: Cambridge University Press.
SHACHAR, Ayelet
2001 *Multicultural Jurisdictions: Cultural Differences and Women's Rights in a Liberal State*. Cambridge: Cambridge University Press.

BOOK REVIEW

Stephen Tierney (ed.), *Accommodating Cultural Diversity*. Aldershot UK and Burlington VT: Ashgate. 2007. ix + 240 pp.

Matthias Koenig and Paul de Guchteneire (eds.), *Democracy and Human Rights in Multicultural Societies*. Aldershot UK and Burlington VT: Ashgate. Paris: UNESCO. 2007. xvii +308 pp.

Prakash Shah and Werner F. Menski (eds.), *Migration, Diasporas and Legal Systems in Europe*. London and New York: Routledge-Cavendish. 2006. xviii + 405 pp.

Gordon R. Woodman

These three collections concern the consequences in law of the multicultural character of the modern state of the North. Thus they consider some of the most prominent topics in current debates about legal policy in these states. Political scientists and sociologists were writing intensively about the nature and consequences of the cultural diversity of modern societies 30 or 40 years ago, at a time when those legal scholars who took account of situations of cultural diversity concentrated on anti-discrimination laws. As in recent years public political debate in countries of the North has been increasingly concerned with the reaction of the state to the phenomenon of cultural diversity, lawyers have been led to examine ever more closely the options of legal policy in this regard.

The debates have been of limited scope and have made limited progress. They have been constrained by a tendency to look exclusively at the state and its laws and policies. They have, moreover, generally ignored the extensive experience of cultural diversity in other regions of the world and at other periods of history. We must hope that this not very fruitful stage will blossom into a fuller, deeper debate in the future. These three books all contribute significantly to the present stage of development, but they illustrate also the limited degree of development so far achieved.

Accommodating Cultural Diversity emerges from a conference organised by the

Centre for Canadian Studies and the School of Law at the University of Edinburgh, and focuses primarily on Canadian experience and questions about Canadian state legal policy. Its object is to

> ... offer a variety of perspectives, both describing how contemporary democracies manage diversity and offering normative prescriptions for how they might better do so (Tierney: 1),

although the possibility of very wide variation in perspective must be viewed with doubt. Six of the ten contributors are law academics, and another is a member of the Department of Justice of Canada.

After the editor's introductory chapter, Part I consists of three chapters on 'the evolving theory of cultural diversity'. Will Kymlicka, the political philosopher whose contribution to this field of theory has been profound and influential, gives an informative general overview of the current 'global diffusion of multiculturalism', while Helder de Schutter and Dwight Newman present critical, constructive papers on Kymlicka's theories. Part II takes 'the case of Aboriginal peoples' and consists of three papers which consider different questions. Avigail Eisenberg's is a discussion with world-wide references of the use of the concept of group identity in claims by Aboriginal peoples. Sonia Harris-Short considers critically how far self-government of Aboriginal groups in Canada tends towards better protection for children. Kathryn Last studies the question of the return to Aboriginal peoples of objects of cultural heritage. The three papers in Part III are concerned with the interpretation of the Canadian constitution in relation to issues of cultural diversity. Mayo Moran is concerned with the varying interpretations by the Supreme Court of the equality guarantee in section 15. Peter Oliver asks how constitutional changes may enable the special identity of Quebec to be satisfactorily reflected. Warren Newman examines the relationship between judicial conceptions of the rule of law and the status of the constitutional text in the context of an increasingly diverse society.

Democracy and Human Rights in Multicultural Societies is a collection of 14 papers published in earlier versions in UNESCO's *International Journal on Multicultural Societies* (*IJMS*) following the Member States' adoption in 2001 of the Universal Declaration of Cultural Diversity. It is not limited to one state, although it focuses overwhelmingly on states of the North. It is stated that

> ...its major aim is to understand, explain and assess public policy responses to ethnic, linguistic and religious diversity (Koenig and de Guchteneire: 3).

The contributors come from a range of disciplines, from academic law through sociology to linguistics.

The editors' introduction contains a wide-ranging survey of current ideas on 'Political Governance of Cultural Diversity', Part I is concerned with 'Ethno-National Movements', that is, on ethnic groups which can feasibly claim that they would be viable political entities were they able to secede from the states within which they are politically incorporated. All those considered are engaged in conflicts, carried on with little or much violence, over their current status. The Part begins with a chapter giving a general theoretical discussion, developed by reference to various instances, including those discussed in the following chapters (Juan Díez-Medrano). These chapters report on and consider the cases of Basque nationalism (Enric Martínez-Herrera), Northern Ireland (StefanWolff) and the Kurdish independence movement in Turkey (Matthew Adam Kocher). Díez-Medrano also discusses briefly Québec and Chiapas, but the papers on these groups published in the *IJMS* are not included in the book. Part II, 'Linguistic Diversity', considers national and international language policy in multi-lingual states. After a study of the legal perspective on language rights as human rights (Fernand de Varennes), there follow chapters on the role of the Organization for Security and Co-operation in Europe in the protection of linguistic minorities (Sally Holt and John Packer), language rights in the Baltic states (Boriss Cilevičs) and South Africa (Kristin Henrard), and the impact of language policies on endangered languages (Suzanne Romaine). Part III is about 'Religious Diversity'. The first chapter here examines the contemporary, global rise of 'fundamentalist and communal-religious movements', and argues that these should be seen as 'the multiplication of different, yet presumably universalistic, interpretations of modernity', not as involving a 'clash of civilizations' (Shmuel N. Eisenstadt). The next examines modes of religious pluralism in the modern, globalizing world (Ole Riis). The last two report on and discuss respectively the new multi-faith approach in prison chaplaincy in England and Wales (James A. Beckford), and religious pluralism in post-Soviet Russia (Kathy Rousselet).

Migration, Diasporas and Legal Systems in Europe does not expressly indicate in its title that it addresses the issues of law in multicultural societies, but by implication, given the nature of the prominent streams of migration in Europe today, it clearly is concerned with these.

> The questions being asked in this volume [are] about what European legal systems have been doing and ought to be doing about these immigration streams (Shah and Menski: 1).

It consists of 19 papers first delivered at a WG Hart Legal Workshop on 'The Challenge of Migration to Legal Systems' at the Institute of Advanced Legal Studies, University of London. All but one of the 23 contributors are lawyers, but a certain variety of approaches follows from the fact that they come from a wide range of different national backgrounds.

The book is not divided by titles into sections, but the editors' Introduction gives a labelling of successive sets of chapters. The first four papers, thus, seek to present a 'long range view ... [of] the structural implications raised for legal systems resulting from significant South-North migration,' that is, the migration which produces in Europe coexistence of different contrasting cultures. Menski in his opening paper argues the case for looking at models from the South of state laws which include the personal laws of different ethnic and religious groups. Roger Ballard, a social anthropologist, recounts details of the cultural experience and 'cultural navigation' strategies of South Asian immigrants to Europe. Mathias Rohe examines the different approaches in European state laws to the Islamic presence. Mohamed M. Keshavjee reports on the Conciliation and Arbitration Boards set up by the Shia Ismaili community to provide dispute settlement procedures in communities in Europe. The next section is concerned with nationality and citizenship. Helen Toner focuses on the introduction of citizenship of the European Union (EU), and the case-law of the European Court of Justice developing it. Nicholas Sitaropoulos studies the Greek law of nationality, Ciara Smyth and Donncha O'Connell developments in Irish citizenship law, and Melanie Smith and Jo Shaw changes in the Lithuanian law of citizenship and their effects on political life.

Almost all the remaining sections focus on migration. The three chapters of the next section are directed at family reunification through immigration, and the related human rights issues. Helena Wray studies the decisions of British entry clearance immigration officials in cases where entry applications are based on the applicant's marriage to a member of an ethnic minority community resident in the UK. Sarah K. van Walsum takes the attitudes of Dutch state officials when migrant mothers decide that their children should be reared in their countries of origin. She examines the impact of the European Court of Human Rights on these cases, while Esther Weizsäcker examines the case-law in general of the court on the entry and residence of aliens. There follows a section concerned with laws affecting migration within the EU. Philippa Gingell-Littlejohn takes issues concerning the ten member states which joined in 2004, and the reluctance to accede to their nationals' claims to rights of migration within the EU. Nathalia Berkowitz and Maria Delgado examine the position of Moroccan migrants in Spain, while Bülent Çiçekli takes Turkish state immigration control, which has been changing as a result of the growing prospects of Turkey's joining the EU. Ryszard Cholewinski critically studies EU immigration law generally, arguing that the lawmakers show insufficient realism regarding the economic issues related to immigration. The next section contains two more specific studies of immigration control systems, one by Fiona Lindsley on that of the UK (of which she has been the Independent Monitor), the other by Gbenga Oduntan on the Juxtaposed Control Systems between Britain and her near neighbours, France, Belgium and the Netherlands, through which many immigrants and would-be immigrants travel. The final section consists of two chapters which study the rather different subject of systems of property law, but relate them to issues of immigration. Anneke Rachel Smit argues, on the basis of research in Kosovo and Georgia, that an international right of return can be frustrated by difficulties in implementing property restitution programmes. Caroline Sawyer shows how in post-communist Bulgaria the pressures of economic globalization on land law has tended to produce conflict and exclusion along ethnic lines.

These three collections undoubtedly provide a wealth of useful contributions to the development of this field of legal pluralism, that is, the study of laws of all types in relation to the multicultural aspect of societies. The papers here do not provide a comprehensive account nor a definitive theorisation (which might of course consist of formulations of competing theories) of the field. The study of this field has not yet reached the stage where such general results can be expected. Far more information is needed, and theories need to be related to that empirical work. A certain proportion of the work presented in these volumes consists of reports of information collected uninformed by much concern with theory. A certain part of the theorising in some papers seems to be unduly formalistic and distanced from any scientifically developed information. However, generally progress is being made, and if the rigour and interest of most contributions can be sustained, the subject will advance.

It is necessary to delimit portions of the field for the purpose of specific studies, but it is important that each such study should be related, as far as possible, to all other parts of the field. Each of these volumes is limited in its scope. It is to be hoped that the particular limitations are not entrenched in the field of study.

The first and obvious limitation is in geographical space. In general *Accommodating Cultural Diversity* is limited to Canada, *Democracy and Human Rights in Multicultural Societies* to the North, and *Migration, Diasporas and Legal Systems in Europe* to Europe. As in any field of comparative legal studies, issues will be illuminated by the greatest possible number and variety of comparable instances. The regions concentrated on in these collections have generally not displayed high, obvious degrees of cultural diversity or of state recognition of differing cultures. Law makers and students in these regions could benefit from the experience of countries in Africa and Asia which have. Even in these overtly limited studies, experience of law and multiculturalism in other regions of the world enhances the papers of contributors such as Ballard and Menski.

The other principal limitation is the restriction to the viewpoint of the state and to policy options available to the state (in which term we may include the supra-state or multi-state entity such as the EU). As the quotations given above show, the collections are directed to the consideration of state 'management' of, or 'response' to, or what the state 'does about' the multicultural character of its population. This is especially dangerous when the tendency of the state is to try to sweep the problem away by decreeing 'assimilation'. The notion of 'accommodation' on the other hand suggests that the state may generously make adjustments to enable cultural diversity to continue to exist. The tendency is the likely result of engaging lawyers to conduct the studies, as has been overwhelmingly done in these volumes. Lawyers generally have expertise only in the doctrines and pronouncements of state laws. They are likely to take as their field of study a state, that is, the entire population over which the state asserts jurisdiction, even if this is a huge population within which there is a multitude of different cultures. They are likely to have little knowledge or empathy with the non-state normative orders effective in the multicultural society, for these are not within their field of expertise. They are likely to respond to any social problem by seeking to formulate the best legal prescriptions on the subject, and to show little inclination to investigate the social reality, either as to the problem aimed at or as to the effects of their laws. More specifically, if state law stipulates 'recognition' of a non-state ethnic or religious normative order, lawyers are likely to assume that the living law (or unofficial law, or customary law) will take effect in state fora. All of these assumptions tend to reduce the possibilities of broad and profound thought on the subject.

It is to be hoped that, after the worthwhile studies in these volumes and others published in the past few years, work in the field will complement these with other approaches, less limited by the tenets of legal positivism and state law pluralism.